FLY TYING
101
A CLASSROOM APPROACH
INSTRUCTOR
CHUCK FOTHERGILL

OTHER BOOKS BY THE AUTHOR:

(co-authored with Bob Sterling)

The Colorado Angling Guide
The Wyoming Angling Guide
The Montana Angling Guide

All Photographs by the Author
Cover Design by the Author
Artwork by Eric Auer
Typesetting by Suzy Sterling
Darkroom Printing by William Meriwether

FLY TYING 101

By: CHUCK FOTHERGILL

STREAM STALKER PUBLISHING COMPANY
Woody Creek, Colorado

First Edition
1 2 3 4 5 6 7 8 9

Published by:
Stream Stalker Publishing
P.O. Box 238
Woody Creek, Colorado 81656

Library of Congress Catalog Card Number: 91-090893

ISBN: 0-9614704-4-5

Printed in the United States of America

DEDICATION

To all fly tying instructors throughout the world who help others learn and appreciate this rewarding skill; and especially to my old friend Jim Poor, whose dedication to fly fishing and fly tying has been an inspiration not only to me, but to a legion of excellent anglers in the Rocky Mountain region.

CONTENTS

INTRODUCTION

I want *you* to possess the skill to tie quality artificial flies! I want them to be durable, symmetrical, properly proportioned, with appealing texture, and a lifelike aura. I want you to be delighted with them, and I want the fish to be seduced by them. I trust that you would want no less than this from your fly tying efforts, and together we can make it happen.

In the back of your mind you probably see visions of being able to tie three or four of your favorite flies within a week's time. Unfortunately this book isn't oriented to satisfy a wish of that magnitude.

This is a book of *how* to tie, not *what* to tie. It's a book of technique, not pattern. I don't clutter your mind with thoughts of tying complete, specific patterns, but rather I want you to concentrate your mental and physical energies to only one thing at a time. In so doing, you'll be skilled enough to tie hundreds of patterns at the end of this "course," not just a few dozen. You'll be able to pick up one of the many fine pattern books available and proceed to tie with confidence. This is a book of solid fundamental technique, not questionable shortcuts. Learning to tie is somewhat like going on a diet or commencing a body-building program; you make slow, but sure, day-to-day progress.

My own introduction to fly tying occurred when I was 15 years old, a high school student in the Midwest, far removed (far to a teenager) from a trout stream. If anyone in my small town taught fly tying, he was unknown to me; so my initial, crude efforts were guided by thin, inadequate little "how-to" manuals and the even thinner pages supplied with my basic fly tying kit.

I imagine the fire that kept me tying, and trying, was fueled by a spark of enthusiasm that never seemed to falter. I would often clamp my vice to the study table in in my college fraternity house, much to the emotionless curiosity of my fraternity brothers; and thereafter I continued this "curious" pastime for fourteen months in my weather-worn canvas tent on a military base in Korea. This particular Asian site of residence offered absolutely no prospects for fishing with the flies I carefully constructed, but it did provide the time necessary to partially fill a shoe box with somewhat crude, certainly colorful, and often oversized "bugs."

It wasn't until after I was discharged and settled at the foot of the Rockies in Denver that I realized my tying skills were grossly inadequate to accommodate the type of fishing I now would be doing. The South Platte River required not only 7X leader points, but also minute #22 and #24 flies. My Midwestern warm water fishing experience hadn't prepared me for the use of these tiny imitations.

Fortunately for me, and many other Denver anglers, fly tying classes were offered periodically by a well-known and highly skilled angler named Jim Poor. In the 1950's Jim and his wife Jane were owners of one of Denver's truly specialized fly fishing shops, known as Mountain View Tackle. Jim was also the region's quintessential tier of trout flies, particularly those tiny, almost imperceptible ones; and his skills were the envy of all who watched him tie, often late into the evening after a full day's work as he filled special orders for anxious customers.

Although quick with a smile or a joke, Jim's basic personality reflected a no-nonsense attitude, and his teaching decorum reflected his personality. It was directed at the very essence of fly construction, and because of his innate practicality and engineering background, he presented the fundamentals of tying in a non-arguable manner.

This book is an attempt in some measure to replicate the feeling I enjoyed in that classroom situation, but more significantly to relay the experience I personally have derived as a teacher of fly tying for many years. This volume will put you into a classroom situation through a succinct, learning-directed text laminated to accompanying photographs which cover all the subtle nuances involved with each interesting slice of fly construction. Many faces of the fly tier's art are presented here, and consequently you'll learn to tie several tails, several bodies, an abundance of hackles, and a variety of wings for dry flies. In addition, you'll learn techniques for tying wet flies, streamers, nymphs, and terrestrials. Many of the techniques are mentioned only once, others are reiterated for reinforcement purposes. Each sentence is carefully worded to prevent ambiguity, so please read slowly and mentally visualize each step in the procedure.

You'll learn the fundamentals of material positioning combined with thread manipulation, executed in the proper sequence to create a desired configuration and texture. The tying sequences set forth here assume you know absolutely nothing about fly tying, so follow through the book page by page, don't jump around. Each page is a foundation, or building block, to the next. Here you will learn the fundamentals from which you can plunge into your own innovation and creative tying in the future. Tying is a personal art to be expressed in our own way, with the materials and colors of our choice.

This writing certainly doesn't pretend to be the "last word" in the technique of elemental fly tying because new discoveries of procedure, materials, and technique are being made every day, and eventually all of us will benefit from that imagination and creativity of our fellow tiers.

This is a book for beginners, people young and older who now look forward to adding a sparkling new facet to their growing knowledge of the precious gem we call flyfishing, just as I sought to learn this new skill over forty years ago.

I really believe this volume will do for you what you hope it will, and I sincerely wish that no matter where you may be fishing, you'll always have with you that "right fly at the right time" because you tied it yourself. Good luck!

Chuck Fothergill
Basalt, Colorado

GETTING STARTED

Your mind is made up, your jaw is set, your determination is fully resolved, and it's time to jump in and get started. No more procrastination, no more just telling yourself you're going to learn to tie flies. This is it. You have the book of instructions in your hand, you know just what table or desk you plan to use, you have or will procure an adequate lamp to illuminate the jaws of your tying vise, but as yet you don't have the vise or the proper scissors or hackle pliers or any of the other tools and materials you'll require in order to experience the genesis of your future as a fly tier. Let's discuss here what tools and materials you'll need to proceed.

Three areas of consideration are required at this juncture. What items do I need? Where can I obtain them, and how much will my budget allow?

How much you'll spend on tools and materials depends on the quantity and quality of items you'll start with. Maybe you'll be able to borrow some tools from a friend; if not, try to buy the best quality you can within the restraints of your budget. If you have a retail tackle or sporting goods store nearby, you have the advantage of inspecting the materials before buying them. Often the best selection and quality will be obtained at those stores which actually specialize in goods for the fly fisherman.

Another source is through mail order catalogs, of which there are several, most of which advertise in those magazines devoted to fly fishing. You can send for these catalogs to determine what each has to offer, and you can usually rely on their products to be of a high quality. Whether you visit a store or review a catalog, you'll be able to form a good idea of what sort of investment is required.

In the area of tools, the greatest disparity of prices is evident when you compare the tying vises. There is a very low end which I can't recommend because they soon become totally inadequate and frustrating to use. The starting point for an adequate vise is near the $25.00 mark, and from here to approximately $50.00 you can find a vise that can serve you well for years to come. You'll also see vises available that cost from $100.00 to $200.00. You'll have to decide whether or not you want equipment in this category at this stage in your tying experience.

In the realm of materials, the most evident price difference is seen among the dry fly hackle necks. The low-end imported necks will range from $10.00 to $15.00, and for the beginner who is doing a lot of practice tying, these are perfectly adequate. As a matter of fact, they were the only type of dry fly necks we had available until just a few years ago when American entrepreneurs started breeding chickens whose feathers were dramatically superior to the imports. These necks range in price from about $35.00 to $60.00 and provide the tier with the very finest of feathers. They are a pleasure to use, but may be more than you wish to consider for the practice exercises in this book.

As for *what* you will need in the way of tools and materials, the following listing includes all the items you'll need to complete the instructions in this volume. None of these items are whimsical, and all are items you can use for your future tying endeavors. Concerning the tools listed, you will want to read Chapter Two to gain some insight into the description and function of each before you purchase them.

One other option is available for the procurement of both tools and materials: the fly tying kit. Kits are assembled to provide a convenient way in which to purchase some basic tools and some basic materials in one handy carton, usually at one economical price. As the saying goes, you receive what you pay for. Often these kits are directed toward economy more than practicality or enduring function, and often they offer such a limited number of tools and materials they need to be supplemented almost immediately. As I said, these kits are put together for the convenience of the purchase; since you are reading this book because you're serious about becoming a good fly tier, I'd suggest you compare bobbins and hackle pliers and vises and other tools needed so you feel good about making the investment in them.

The following list includes those items you'll need to progress completely through this book:

TOOLS (see detailed explanation in Chapter Two)

Vise
Tying Scissors
Bobbin
Hackle Pliers
Hackle Guards
Hackle Gauge
Bodkin
Material Clip
Thompson Style Whip Finisher

TOOLS - optional, but desirable

Hair Stacker
Razor Blade
Tweezers
Thread Twister

HOOKS (Usually can be purchased in less than lots of 100; minimum quantities are indicated)

Mustad #94840	Size 8	For dry flies (20-50)
Mustad #94840	Size 12	For dry flies (100)
Mustad #79580	Size 2	For wet flies (10-20)
Mustad #79580	Size 8	For wet flies (20-50)
Mustad #94831	Size 8	For dry flies (10-20)
Mustad #37160	Size 14	A Bait Hook (10-20)

FEATHERS

Hackle Neck, Dry, Brown
Mallard Breast, Dyed Lemon
Peacock Tail Feather, Eyed
Pheasant Tail Feather, Long
Mallard Wing Quill, Grey, one pair
Ostrich Plume, White
Partridge Hackle, Brown (or substitute)
Turkey Wing Quills, Mottled Brown, one pair (or substitute)

FUR

Hare's Mask, Natural
Muskrat Fur
Miscellaneous, Black & Cream

HAIR

Bear Hair, Brown
Bucktail, Natural
Deer Body Hair, Natural
Kip Tail, White
Moose Body Hair
Squirrel Tail, Red Fox

BODY MATERIAL

Thread, 3/0, Grey
Thread, 6/0, Brown
Yarn, Polypropylene, Grey
Yarn, Polypropylene, Yellow
Chenille, Black
Floss, 4-strand, Red
Yarn, Wool, Brown

Wire, Gold
Wire, Lead, one amp.
Tinsel, Gold, Narrow

MISCELLANEOUS

Plastic Bag, Clear
Bee's Wax
Head Cement
Paraffin
Wax, Thompson's
Monofilament, 5# Test
Monofilament, 15# Test
Monofilament, Flat, Clear, 18# Test
Mylar Piping, Gold

Note: Some of the above items will serve you well for years to come; others might be used for the exercises in this book and used rarely thereafter. I suggest that you purchase them in small quantities: a piece of animal tail rather than the complete tail, a small spool or card of yarn, rather than a skein, a piece of fur rather than a skin. These small quantities will be displayed as such in a store and will be so designated in a catalog, so try not to purchase a lifetime supply before you know you'll be using them for a lifetime!

THE HOOKS WE USE

As fly tiers we are fortunate to be able to build our creations upon a skeletal structure of extremely simple design. Our dressings of fur, feather and thread, though seemingly intricate and complex, are, after all, but a series of several individual applications of material to a straight length of wire. When tying fresh water flies, usually this length does not exceed 3/4 of an inch. We are not required to bend, shape, solder, or weld the backbone of our imitations. Our task at the outset, therefore, is immeasurably simplified over that of other craftsmen whose efforts with metal are much more complex.

"A hook is just a hook," we might say, but is it really? It's true that when we look at a "fish hook" we know what it is, and the purpose for which it was produced. But there are subtle differences in the hooks we use, and I want to discuss those differences now, before we actually put one in our vise and start the tying procedures.

Hooks have several characteristics which are more or less important depending on how seriously we take our tying efforts. As we progress together through this book, our efforts will develop and our interest will strengthen to the point where the use of the proper hook will be fundamental to each type of fly we tie.

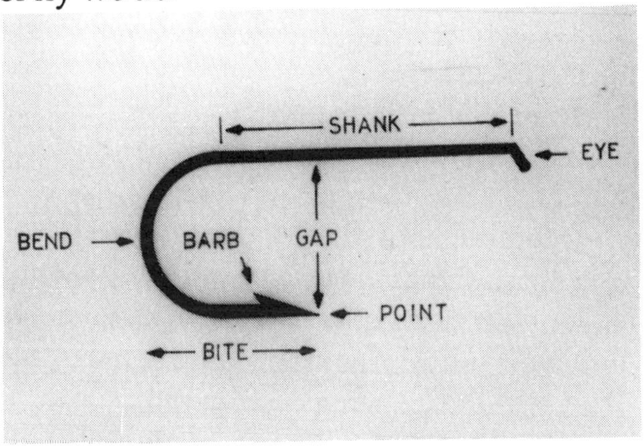

1

First of all, let's learn hook nomenclature. PHOTO 1 describes the hook and how we refer to it when tying flies. These terms are used often throughout the book, and are common-sense enough to be easily learned. Hooks are produced in several countries, including the U.S., Great Britain, Japan and Norway. From the tier's point of view, the greatest variety of sizes and styles are produced by O. Mustad and Son, of Oslo,

Norway. We shall therefore limit our tying to their hooks only.

On each box of 100 hooks, there are listed certain characteristics of the hooks contained within. Not all of the characteristics are listed, however, so I will enumerate on them below. To maintain a continuity throughout this description, we'll use just one hook, which will be the most commonly used dry fly hook.

A - STYLE NUMBER

Just as individual cameras, toasters, and typewriters have their own individual style, or model numbers, so do fish hooks. Each hook of a single style number will have identical characteristics. The only difference between hooks of the same style will be their size, so if you mention only the style number and size when purchasing hooks, you'll know exactly what you're receiving. In this discussion we'll refer to Mustad hook style #94840, a dry fly hook.

B - HOOK SIZE

To meet the demands of tying flies representing different insects in different stages of their life cycles, we must have at our disposal a selection of hooks in different sizes. These sizes are designated by even numbers and for most of our tying efforts will range between number 2 and 22; the size 2 hook being quite large, and the 22 being quite small.

For saltwater fly fishing, hook size designations such as 1/0, 2/0 and 3/0 are used and these hooks are progressively larger than the #2. Tiny trout flies are tied on sizes 24, 26 and 28 which are progressively smaller than the #22. The greatest majority of artificial flies is probably tied for trout fishing, and I would guess the most used sizes are 14, 16, 18 and 20 because the majority of natural insects we imitate are represented with these four sizes.

Bear in mind that the length of the hook shank does not determine the size designation of the hook. The gap determines the size and even though you might compare hooks of dramatically different length, if the gaps are the same then the hook size designation is the same. All size #14 hooks have an identical gap measurement irrespective of the total length of the hook.

C - SHANK LENGTH

To accommodate the divergent physical structure of the many aquatic and terrestrial creatures we imitate, we utilize hooks of different shank length. Within the same size of hook, different styles can have different shank length. In addition to a "regular" length shank, hooks are also designated "short shank" (ss) or "long shank" (ls). In addition to the suffix ss and ls, numbers are used to describe just how extra (x) short or how extra long a particular hook is. For instance, our #94840 hook is, in fact, a 1xls hook. This means the shank is but slightly longer than a "regular" length shank. The larger the number designation, the longer the shank. A 4xls is quite long, a 6xls is very long, and an 8xls is extremely long, and used very rarely. Short shank hooks are likewise designated. A 1xss is slightly shorter than regular, but a 6xss is very short indeed.

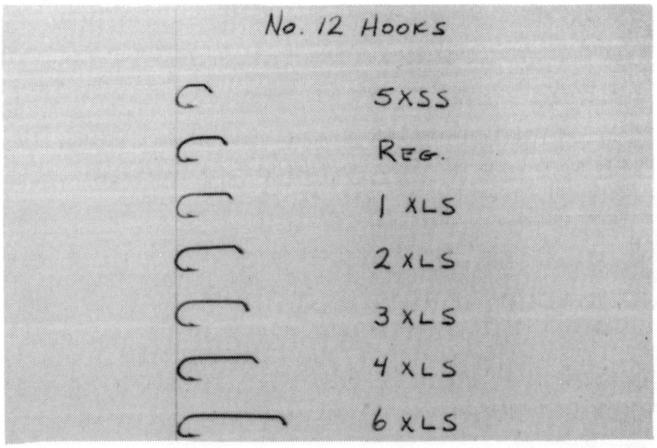

2

Please appreciate that the above are nontechnical descriptions intended only to relay a general comprehension of shank length relationships, not a precise mathematical comparison. PHOTO 2 should relay an understanding far better than any additional words. Though all are size #12 hooks, they all have different style numbers.

D - HOOK FINISH

Hooks are either made of a metal which resists corrosion or are plated with a corrosion-resistant substance. Most hooks, such as our #94840, are called "bronzed" hooks. The rust-fighter here is a brown color, and this finish is most common among trout fly hooks. Hooks used for salmon egg fishing are usually "gold plated." Hooks with a finish which appears black are called "Japanned" hooks and are commonly used in tying Atlantic salmon patterns.

Those hooks which are exposed to the extremely corrosive effects of salt water are either zinc plated or made entirely from stainless steel. Underneath the protective coatings on most hooks is a steel which can rust if the finish is worn or scraped from the hook.

E - THE FORGED HOOK

Without some previous experience with hooks, it's easy to assume that the shank of all hooks is round in cross-section. The #94840 hook, is, in fact, flat on the sides of the shank and bend of the hook. This wire is called forged. The top and bottom of the wire is rounded and the dimensions reveal more steel in the vertical plane than in the horizontal plane, which results in greater strength vertically, the direction on which most pressure is applied to the hook wire when fighting a fish.

F - THE HOLLOW POINT

Most flies are tied on hooks which have points designated as "hollow." Again, the #94840 has this characteristic. The initial impression one has when hearing this term is that there is an empty space within the barb of the hook, as if the barb were crafted from a tubular piece of steel. Such a miraculous machining marvel is not the case. The hollow terminology merely indicates that the top edge of the barb, or spear, is concave, or hollowed out, to reduce resistance as the barb penetrates the fish's mouth.

This point differs from a "straight point" in that the latter has a barb whereon the line extended from the point to the barb tip is a straight line rather than a concave one.

G - THE BEND

The hook in PHOTO 1 illustrates an example of what is referred to as a "perfect bend." Essentially this means the curvature of the bend corresponds to a section of a circle. It is not oval or squareish, but round. The #94840 has this type of bend.

Many other types of bends are manufactured, but there are two with which you should be familiar at this stage even though they are used much less frequently than the perfect bend. The first is the "sproat bend." It differs from the perfect in that the top of the curve is somewhat flattened down. The second is the "limerick bend" and it offers an even greater flattened effect than the sproat.

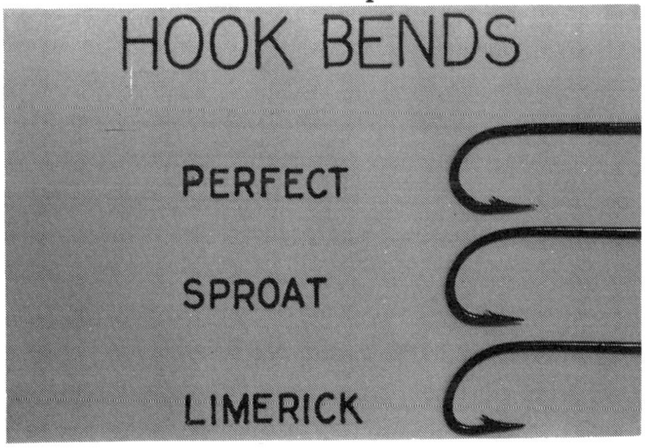

3

My personal choice for most hooks is the perfect bend as I feel it allows the hook to penetrate more deeply into the lip of the fish, and therefore increases the probability that the fish will stay hooked until landed. The more the top of the hook is flattened downward, the more the wire acts as a "bumper" and will restrict penetration. PHOTO 3 illustrates this explanation.

H- OFFSET POINTS

Some hooks are manufactured with the point and barb bent out to the side of the shank when viewed from the top of the hook. When the bend is to the right of the head it is called a reversed bend. To the left is called a kirbed bend. Neither of these hook types is commonly used by the fly tier. Instead, we use what is called a straight bend, where the hook point and barb are positioned directly under the shank. Such is the case with the #94840 and will be the case with all the hooks used in this book except the English bait hook which has a configuration all its own and is used only for certain patterns.

I - WIRE SIZES

Some flies float and some flies sink, and hook makers take these differences into consideration when designing and producing their product. The diameter of the wire used in the hook is obviously going to have a great effect on whether the finished product will sink or float. The manner in which we use our materials while dressing the fly has the greatest effect on whether or not it floats, but being rational and reasonable individuals, we must also consider the amount of steel used in the hook.

All hook wire is not the same gauge, but rather it varies in diameter from what is referred to as "regular" wire. We may think of regular wire as being average in diameter, and from this point of reference, the wire can be "extra fine" or even "3 extra fine" (3x fine). On the larger side, wire is referred to as "stout" or maybe "2x stout." Our #94840 is an extra fine wire, and logically so, because the hook is intended for use on floating flies. The regular and stout wire hooks are used on sinking flies.

J - HOOK EYES

There are four commonly used terms in describing the eyes of hooks with which we should be familiar.

1. **Ball Eye**

The wire diameter of this eye is the same as that of the hook shank. It is bent either up or down or extends straight off the shank.

2. **Tapered Eye**

This description refers to the fact that the wire which is circularly bent to form the hook eye tapers progressively from the shank itself to the very end of the wire where it butts against the shank to close the eye. This tapering is not only more delicate than the ball eye and offers a smaller profile to the view of the fish, but to some degree is lighter in weight, thus increasing its floating capability.

3. **Turned Down Eye**

This eye is abbreviated by the letters TDE. It is very common to fly hooks and is most generally a tapered eye. The #94840 hook has a turned down tapered eye.

4. **Turned Up Eye**

Abbreviated as TUE, some hooks possess this type of eye. I personally have no particular affinity for it except in the smaller sizes, from #18 down. (When comparing hook sizes, "down" means the hook is physically smaller although its size number is larger.) My preference for TUE hooks in the tiny sizes is because I feel the hook has a greater chance for getting into the fish's lip by having the eye turned up out of the way rather than aiming downward and acting as a bumper against the lip. This problem is not so apparent in the larger sizes where the distance between the point and the eye is considerably greater.

THE THREADS WE USE

To use one type of tying thread for all types of flies makes as little sense as using one pattern of fly for all angling situations. In this brief section we'll discuss the threads we use and gain enough understanding of each to be able to choose the right thread at the right time.

When we determine what size and pattern of fly we wish to tie, one of our first considerations will be what thread we'll use. Assuming we have a variety of threads from which to choose, we take into account two different factors: strength and color.

Back in the "old days," prior to the 1970's, most of the tying thread used was made of silk and references in the tying manuals appropriately used the term "tying silk." The advantage of silk thread over a mercerized cotton was a greater strength to diameter ratio and a harder finish when wound to build up the proper diameter of the tapered head. It absorbed head cement well and was manufactured in very small diameters. These silk thread sizes were designated by "aught" numbers such as four-aught or six-aught as are the threads of today, and are written as follows: 4/0 or 6/0. The smallest was designated as 8/0. Most trout fly tying then was done with 5/0 and 6/0 because of the greater strength they provided. Unfortunately the colors available were limited to black and white.

Today's tier has the option of drawing from a much broader range of quality threads made almost exclusively of strong synthetic materials under a variety of trade names. Also available now is a wide selection of colors to accommodate the most demanding tier, and they can be obtained in sizes to match the requirements of tiny trout patterns as well as the more substantial salt water dressings. A rough breakdown of thread sizes to use for designated hook sizes is as follows:

8/0 - #18 to #28
6/0 - #12 to #16
5/0 - #10 to #14
4/0 - #8 and #10
3/0 - #6 and #8
2/0 - #2 to #6

My general preference regarding thread color is to utilize one which matches the general color of the fly. Tan thread on a tan fly, black thread on a blackish fly, grey on a greyish pattern, etc. Certain patterns do call for specific colors, particularly on the head of the fly, but there's also plenty of latitude for the tier to choose the color he prefers. Tan, grey and black cover most situations.

The catalogs and retail stores usually offer several types of threads from which to choose, and I recommend you purchase three or four different types and try them. Experience will quickly teach you which thread you prefer for the types and sizes of flies you are tying.

The last point which should be brought out here has to do with applying wax to the thread. Most threads are available pre-waxed from the manufacturer, but some must be waxed after purchase. Bee's wax, available in cake form, is rubbed or melted onto the thread for several reasons. First, it helps prevent the tiny fibers from fraying under normal use. Second, the wax acts as a binder, or adhesive agent, to which materials can adhere. Wax also prevents the thread from slipping laterally on the hook shank which could cause an unwanted repositioning of materials. When thread is purchased un-waxed, it's a simple procedure to simply rub the cake of bee's wax, or manufactured substitute, against the thread after it has been initially attached to the hook shank.

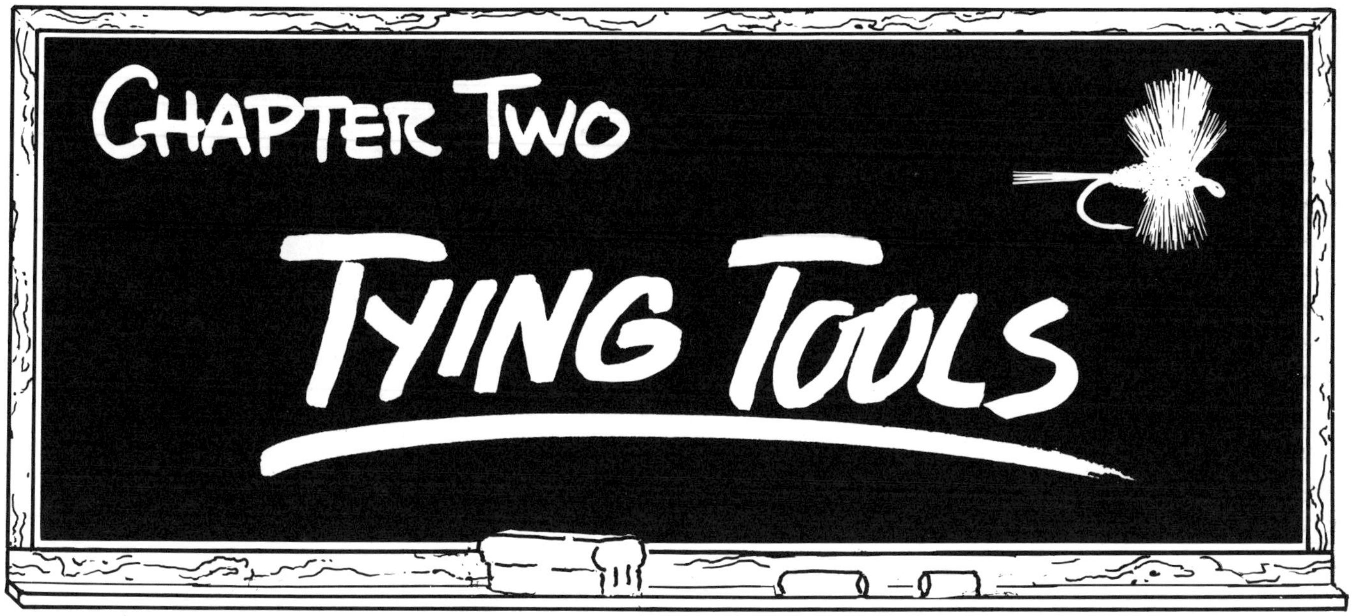

It's difficult to imagine any art or craft in which its purveyors don't utilize one or more basic tools unique to their particular efforts to simplify their special tasks. Fly tying is no exception, and though the tools we use look unusual and exotic to the uninitiated, they serve important functions toward the completion of neat and durable flies.

Because I learned tying with the use of tools, I continue to use them. There are some tiers, however, who manually accomplish operations for which a tool may also be utilized. The choice of methods we use are, of course, the result of personal preference and I would never claim that an experienced tier should change his or her ways. I do believe, however, that the beginner who starts his tying career utilizing the various tools available, will ultimately prefer their use over manual techniques.

In the photographs to follow I have tried to display more than one design of each tool described, but the photos do not compare the many tools available from all manufacturers. Some of the items are homemade and if they function well, they are merely a reflection of the tier's inventiveness and desire to add a personal touch to his tying bench. Although some tools of a specific type could be considered better than others, there is no singularly "perfect" tool which *all* tiers should use. As with other types of equipment, eventually the user tries several and chooses his particular favorite. And so it should be!

If there are 5,000 fly tiers in a given region, there are probably also 5,000 different methods of organizing their tying tables. I don't intend to offer any layouts or descriptions herein, because each individual will design his own and probably change it periodically as he accumulates more experience, ideas and equipment. I would like to offer one suggestion, however, beyond the obvious conclusion that the layout of your equipment and materials should provide for convenience. Those tools with sharp points or cutting edges should be kept secure from the curiosity of children and pets, and any materials which have a real or sentimental value should be treated likewise. Having been a retailer of tying materials for a number of years, I've heard many tales of woe relating the disastrous outcome when playful pets had nothing better to do than chew up a favorite, and not inexpensive, hackle neck.

As skill and interest in tying increase, so does our inventory of materials. Eventually our one shoe box will no longer accommodate the supply of furs and feathers and threads and hooks we have accumulated, and additional boxes find their place on the tying table or bookcase shelf or closet floor. In my case, all three of the above apply! Some tiers prefer cedar boxes; some prefer large glass bottles; some use plastic bags or plastic boxes.

Whatever the container used, consideration must be given to possible exposure to moths and mice. With furs and feathers in particular, sealed containers are highly recommended and the use of moth crystals is encouraged. I know one retailer of tying materials who stores his hackle necks in his basement in 50-gallon steel drums. An oil drum in the corner of your den isn't what I'm suggesting here, but a reasonable degree of protection to valued materials is a precaution which should be seriously considered.

In describing the tools we use, I will separate them into two categories—essential and optional. There may be tiers who read this section and feel that some of the essentials should be optionals, and vice versa. I personally use all of the tools described, but if I were traveling and had to leave some tools behind, they would be those in the optional category. For the beginner, however, all the essential tools should be available for use at your tying table.

ESSENTIAL TOOLS

A - FLY TYING VISE

The fly tying vise is available in many forms, from extremely basic and inefficient, to relatively complex and sometimes over-designed. PHOTO 4 shows a variety of styles.

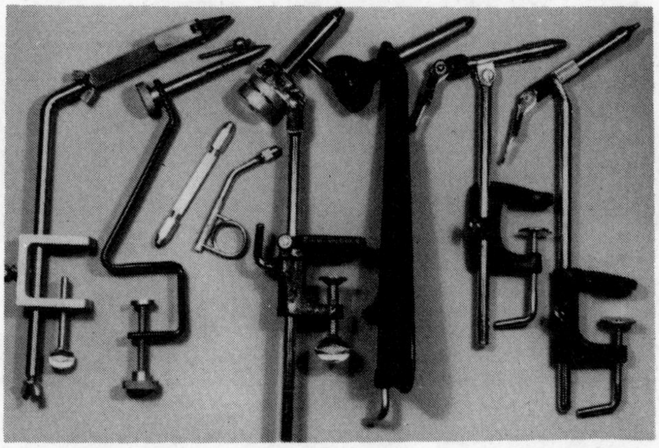

4

The most important factor to look for in a vise is the holding power of the jaws for a wide range of hook sizes. In other words, the jaws must separate wide enough to accommodate a hook of large diameter wire, and hold it securely; but it must also be delicate enough to grip the smallest of hooks and hold them conveniently and securely. Not all vises perform these two important functions, so when shopping for a vise, consider the holding performance of the jaws as well as the following characteristics:

1. Are the metal parts of the vise which come into contact with the hands and thread smooth to the touch? Or are they so rough they'll possible fray or cut the tying thread?

2. Is the mechanism which opens and closes the jaws easy and convenient to operate?

3. Is the height of the jaws adjustable in relation to the surface of the table? This is particularly important to people taller or shorter than average.

4. Will the vise mount firmly to the table and remain solidly positioned during the pressures applied to the hook while tying?

5. Does the vise have a rotating sleeve? In

other words, does it offer the capability of turning the hook upside-down without removing the hook from the jaws?

6. Is it convenient (or even possible) to mount a material clip to the vise?

7. If you're left-handed, will it mount on the table and function easily in the left-handed position?

8. Do the component parts seem strong and capable of continued, trouble-free use for a period of several years?

This listing presents a critical analysis of possible vise characteristics. Not all of the items are absolutely necessary, but obviously the more of them having importance to you personally, the happier you'll be with the tool.

B - SCISSORS

As with the vise, scissors also come in several shapes and sizes, PHOTO 5. The price of the scissors is normally a good indicator of their quality, but other characteristics are also important.

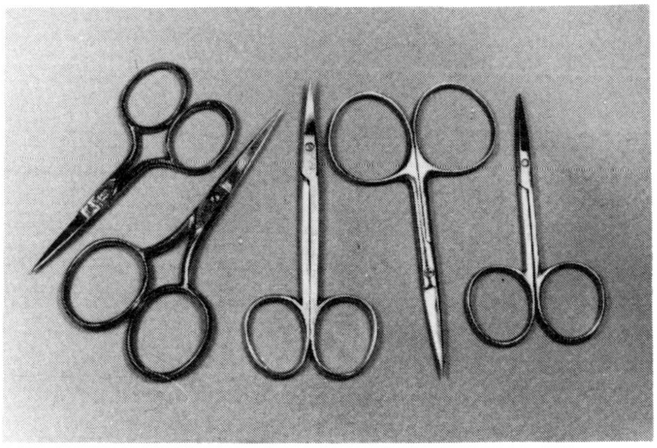

5

1. Are the finger holes large enough to comfortably accommodate your thumb? They should be!

2. Is the over-all length of the scissors short enough to stay out of the way when tying with the scissors *in* your hand?

3. Are the blades durable enough to cut through a bundle of hair, yet delicate enough to snip off a single wisp or fiber of a feather?

4. Do the very tips of the blades cut well? A great deal of cutting is done with the last 1/8 inch of the blade tips, so assure they cut to the very end by first trying them on a piece of paper.

5. Do you want straight blades or curved blades? For most tying, tiers prefer the straight blades and that's what I would recommend as your first pair. You may eventually also want a pair with curved blades as they are very convenient for cutting hair into a round, conical shape, such as on deer hair bass bugs, imitation mice and frogs, and the heads of muddler minnows.

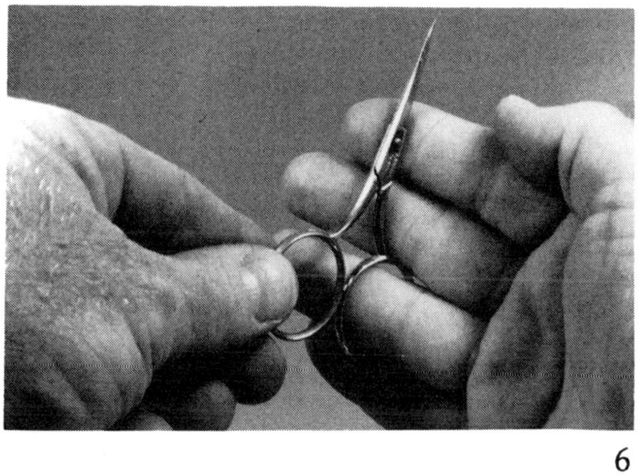

6

I want to stress here the wisdom of holding the scissors in the hand (the right hand for right-handed tiers) throughout the entire process of tying a fly. It's easy to do, will feel very natural after some practice, and will save you considerable tying time. PHOTO 6 shows how the scissors are placed on the hand and PHOTO 7 shows them in position, but out of use, while tying the fly.

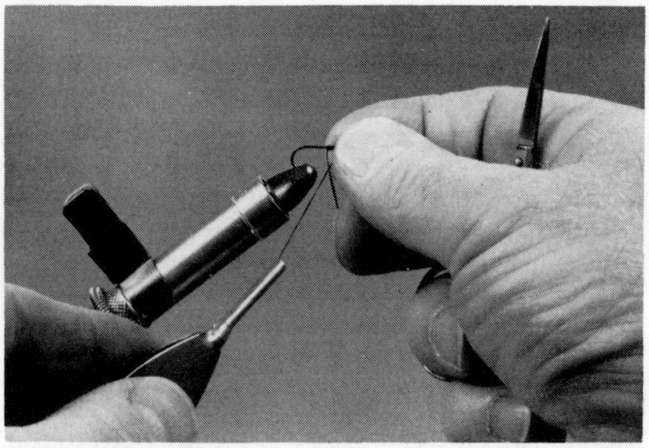

7

Scissors may be used up to a dozen times on each fly tied. Picking them up from the table and setting them down again that many times can consume considerable time that could otherwise be used for actual tying. Even for those to whom time is of no importance, the convenience may be a positive consideration. At least give this technique a try and judge for yourself.

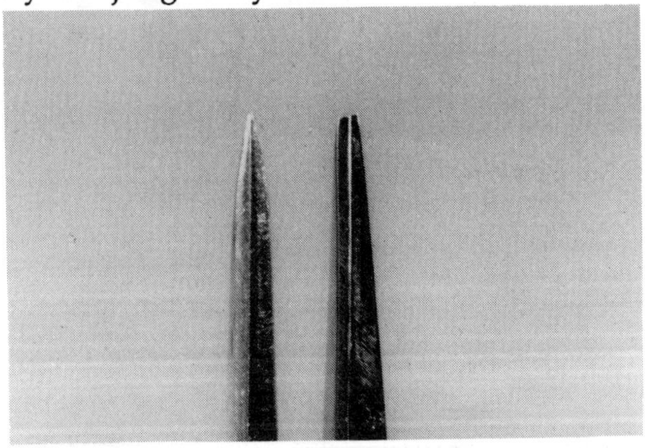

8

Once you have obtained your scissors, do the following procedures before you start using them. First, rub the tips of the scissors against a magnet. This will magnetize them and make the picking up of hooks no problem at all. Secondly, I suggest you bevel the *sides* of the points by rubbing them on emery paper or a knife sharpening stone. When new, the tips are blunt, or square, across the tips. This condition will not allow you to get in very close when cutting on small flies. PHOTO 8 makes a comparison of a new pair against one that has been beveled.

C - THE BOBBIN

I mean no offense to the many excellent tiers who prefer not to use a bobbin, but I personally find tying without one to be less efficient, more inconvenient, and more time consuming than tying with one.

The bobbin is that device which holds the spool of thread while tying, and it is available in a variety of forms, PHOTO 9. All commercial bobbins with which I'm familiar are designed to hold the wood or plastic spool onto which the thread is wound by the manufacturer. The most efficient of these, I feel, is the wishbone shape which has two spring wires attached at one end to the tube and two spheres, or half spheres, at the other end to press into the holes on either side of the thread spool. It is important that these bobbins have as little bulk as possible, have a good capability for adjusting the tension against the spool, and have no rough edges which could catch and tear the thread.

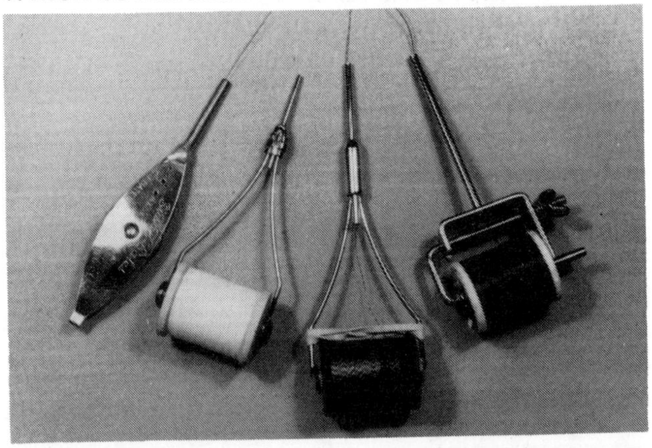

9

My personal preference in bobbins is one which is not available through normal sources. This bobbin is of the "homemade" variety and to the best of my knowledge is the creation of Jim Poor. Aside from being a master fly tier, angler par excellence, and a former owner of Anglers All, Ltd., a tackle shop in

Littleton, Colorado, Jim is also an innovator of equipment for the angler. This particular bobbin consists of a brass or copper tube soldered to a tatting shuttle. Extra metal spools for these shuttles are available and any number of threads can be transferred from their original spools to the shuttle spools and used in one bobbin frame. My personal bobbin arsenal includes about 20 of these homemade bobbins and an additional 20 spools wound with a variety of threads in different sizes and colors.

The thread can be easily transferred from the original spool by securing the metal spool to a bolt with a nut, inserting the bolt into the jaws of an electric drill, attaching the thread to the metal spool and pulling the trigger. I press bee's wax against unwaxed thread as the transfer is being made, and allow the original spool to rotate on a nail driven into an appropriate place. The transfer of 50 yards of thread takes less than two minutes.

The style of bobbin used is not as important as the fact that one *is* used. Its use has several advantages over thread which is hand-held while tying.

1. After each tying step, the bobbin merely hangs by the thread from the hook shank. The weight of the bobbin provides proper tension so that materials do not change position. Hand-held threads must be secured to another device to maintain such tension.

2. The winding of thread to the hook shank can be done much more accurately because it comes from the solid end of a metal tube rather than the soft, curved ends of fingers.

3. Rough fingertips, which many of us have to one degree or another, can fray and weaken thread, whereas the smooth tube will not.

4. Without the use of a bobbin, the length of thread required for any fly must be estimated, then cut from the spool before tying. An underestimate is obviously inconvenient; an overestimate is wasteful. No estimate, no inconvenience and no waste is necessary when using a bobbin.

Silk and rayon floss also come from the manufacturer wound on wood spools of the same size as thread and the wishbone type bobbin can be used to wind floss bodies, particularly if your fingers are rough and might tend to fray the floss.

The threading of a bobbin is relatively simple and can be accomplished in one of two ways. The first requires nothing but the tier's ability to inhale. After the spool is mounted securely between the arms of the bobbin, pull off a length of thread six to eight inches long. Place the end of thread up the bottom end of the tube as far as possible, and suck strongly on the tip of the tube. The thread should now be in your mouth and the bobbin ready for use!

After a bobbin has been used for some time, the base of the tube may accumulate a layer of wax from the thread and offer problems to the inhaling method. If it does, double over a piece of wire or nylon monofilament, push the loop through the tube from tip to base, insert the thread through the loop, and pull thread up and out of the tip of the tube.

Tension on the spool should allow the spool to rotate with a smooth, but firm, pull on the thread. If tension is adjusted too tightly, the thread will most likely break or the hook will bend. If tension is too loose, adequate pressure to hold materials in place when winding will be insufficient.

Care should always be exercised while tying not to drop the bobbin onto a rough floor. A concrete floor in particular can scar the tip of the tube very badly and the slightest rough burr can weaken and break even the heaviest of thread. Such burrs can be removed and adequate polish returned to the tube by applying an abrasive compound to a wood kitchen match, inserting the match into the jaws of an electric drill and allowing the drill to spin the abrasive against the tube tip. The process may be a bit tedious, but it is effective.

D - HACKLE PLIERS

I assume all tiers use this tool. Their function remains the same, though styles and sizes differ considerably, PHOTO 10. They grip the tips of feathers as the feathers are wound around the shank of a hook to form a hackle. Such feathers are not wound on every fly we tie, but are certainly used on all the types of flies we tie—wets, dries, streamers, nymphs, terrestrials, etc. Therefore I consider the tool a must for every tier.

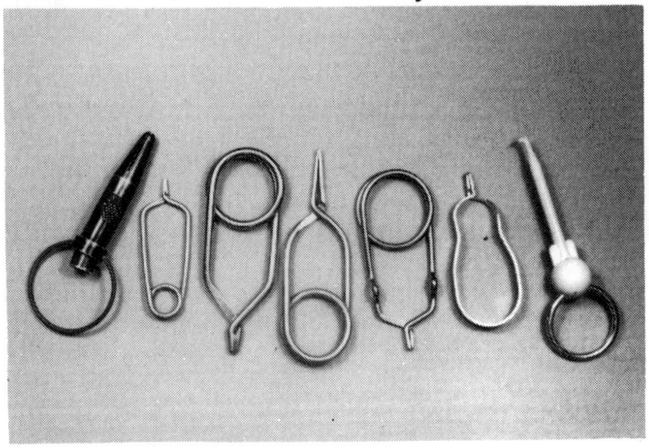

10

Some distinct disadvantages are evident if we choose to hold these feathers with our fingers instead of pliers:

1. Some feathers are just too small to grasp well with our relatively large, soft, and curved fingertips.

2. If the feather is large enough to grasp, the grip is not always positive, and unplanned releases of the feather are frequent.

3. Because of the configuration of our fingertips, we must grasp too much of a small feather to allow an adequate number of turns to accomplish our goal.

4. Winding a finger-held feather may not produce the accuracy required which routinely is attained with the use of pliers. This is particularly true when tying small sizes.

My personal requirements in pliers are as follows:

1. The jaws must make a tight grip on the feather fibers or quill across the entire tip of the jaws, not just in the middle. I don't like the erratic unreliability of pliers having a rubber pad on one jaw.

2. The tool must have a finger hole large enough to allow insertion of my index finger up to the first knuckle with enough spare room to allow the hole to rotate around the finger.

3. The jaws should be straight across and flush in length. Jaws which have rounded tips require too much "centering" on the feather. Jaws which are not flush are not necessarily inefficient, but they do promote an unnecessary aggravation, similar to cutting with scissors having one blade shorter than the other.

4. A recommendation is needed here concerning the pressure it requires to open the jaws of some new pliers. It's not uncommon with a few models to be startled at the amount of force required to open them. If you like the pliers but can't operate them conveniently, try these two suggestions:

a. Rather than squeezing with your thumb and index finger, and having the pliers slip out of your fingers because of the strong pressure required, put your index finger between the side wires and squeeze with your thumb and middle finger, PHOTO 11.

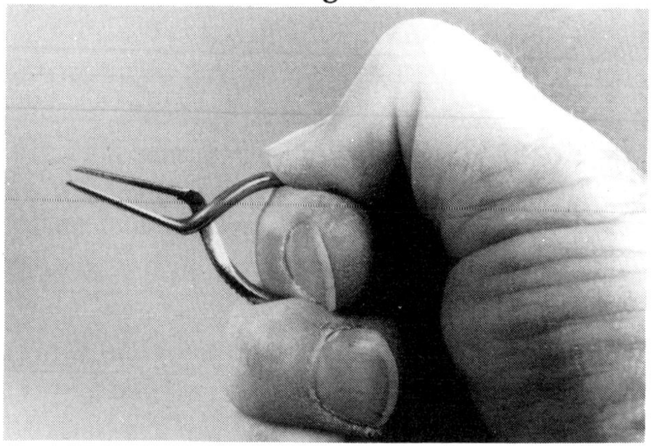

11

b. Considerable resistance to your squeezing efforts can be relieved if the side wires are squeezed to their limit a few times with a pair of household pliers, PHOTO 12.

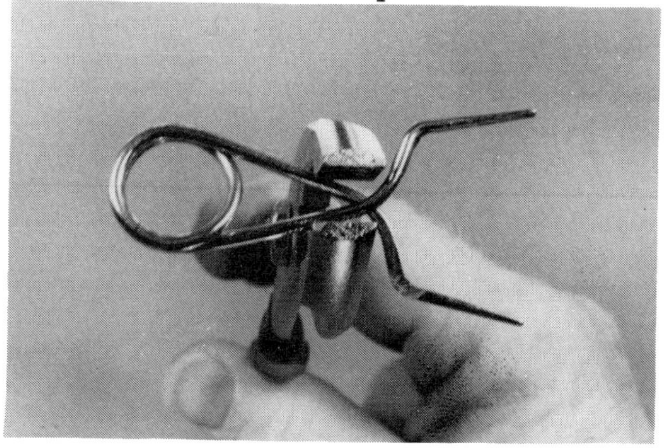

12

Some new pliers have very sharp edges on the tips of the jaws. If you find your feathers are being severed by these edges, merely smooth them off with a piece of fine-grit emery cloth.

E - HACKLE GUARDS

These tools are usually sold as a set of component parts including a string, a weight and three cup-shaped guards, each having a center hole of different diameter to be used on hooks of different sizes, PHOTO 13. When the fly (usually a dry fly) is complete except for winding the head, this tool is used. The guard holds the hackle fibers out of the way so a whip finish knot can be tied without interference from these fibers.

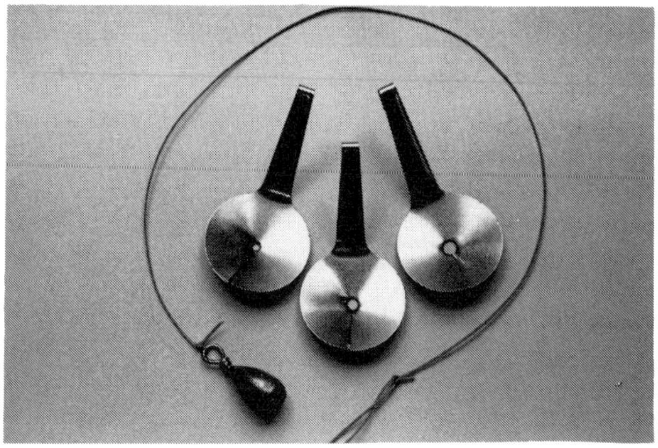

13

F - THE HACKLE GAUGE

This simple tool is seldom used by experienced tiers, but is an important aid to the beginner. Its sole purpose is to assist the tier in choosing a feather of the proper size to use in hackling a standard dry fly. Because proportions are important to this type of fly, we want the hackle length to be reasonably close to what is accepted as correct. We can make guestimates and use trial and error to find the right feather, but the tool saves us time and material.

Several gauges are available, PHOTO 14, and some provide more than just hackle size, so the choice of this tool can be up to the tier. They'll all do the job.

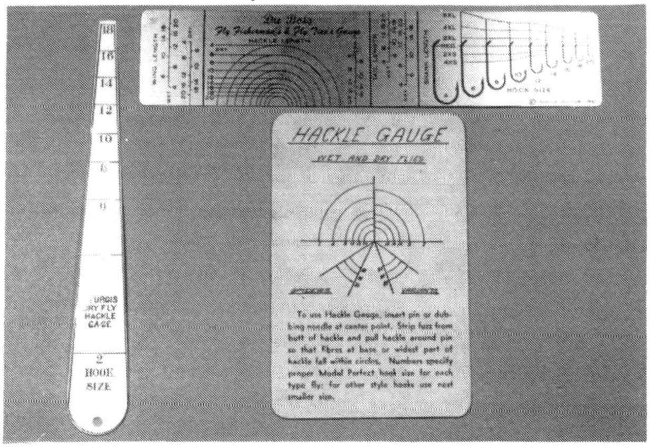

14

G - THE BODKIN

Also referred to as a Bodkin Point, this tool is extremely simple, yet serves three valuable functions:

1. Its use is almost a must in applying cement or varnish to the heads of flies.

2. It is used to good advantage in picking out parts of flies which occasionally become inadvertently tied down in an improper position.

3. When we desire the body of a fly, usually a nymph pattern, to be rough and fuzzy, we can accentuate this condition by plucking up the fibers of the body material with the bodkin point.

As seen in PHOTO 15, this tool can be made with a variety of handles, including a common cork. Part of the handle, however, should have a flat surface to prevent it from rolling around on, or off, the table.

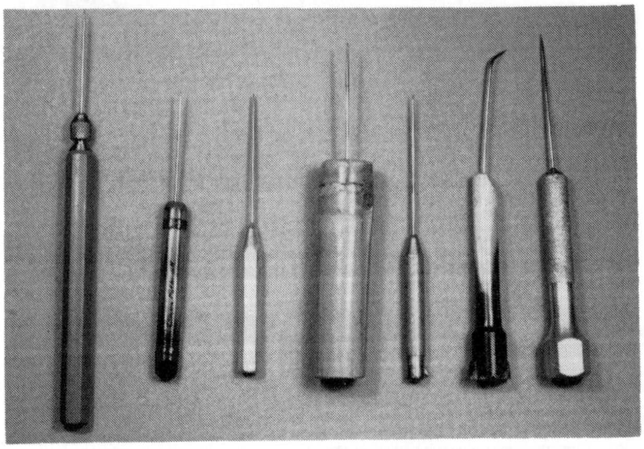

15

H - THE WHIP FINISHER

A whip finish knot on the head of a fly is absolutely necessary for durability. It may be tied either with the fingers alone, or with the use of this tool. Some tiers use it, some don't. So be it! Both methods produce the same final result. I personally use the tool because I can tie the knot more efficiently and more quickly than tying it with my fingers only.

The most widely used whip finisher and the one I recommend is pictured in the middle of PHOTO 16. Its total length is approximately 6 inches, and its use, as with the other tools in this chapter, will be described later in the text. This particular finisher is manufactured in a standard and small size. These designations have to do only with the size of the tip of the tool, not its overall dimensions, and the small size does well on just about all hook sizes you will tie. Large size flies such as might be used in salmon or saltwater fishing, are better tied with the standard size tool.

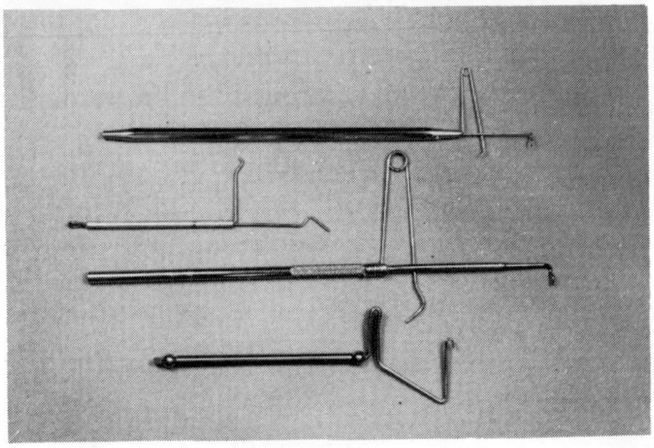

16

I - A TABLE LAMP

Strained eyes are not the goal of the fly tier, whether amateur or professional. Tying on a poorly lit vise is a sure road to eye strain and less than satisfactory tying results. I prefer a small table lamp, taking up as little space as possible on the tying table, but providing a strong beam of light on the jaws of the vise and the hook. Lamps having high and low switch positions seem to work very well when used in the high position. I've seen many lamps with only one switch position and they don't seem to emit enough light for comfortable tying.

I am right handed and want the beam of light to come toward the hook from the right side, or toward the eye of the hook. This light direction makes sense because the majority of a fly is tied from left to right (for a right hander) and the light rays are beamed on what we are now doing, not what we have already done. The arm of the lamp must be long enough to allow positioning of the lamp shade far enough above the hook to permit us to wind thread and materials without hitting the shade with our hand, bobbin or hackle pliers.

J - THE MATERIAL CLIP

This simple device attaches to the arm, or sleeve, of the vise and remains there essentially forever as there is no reason to remove it. In PHOTO 17 the upright clip on the right and the spring clip on the left are available through most suppliers of tying tools and materials. The function of the clip is to hold back out of the way those materials such as wire, tinsel, thread, floss, etc. which must be tied into the fly at an early step in its construction, but not actually wound around the shank until a later time. The most common usage of the clip is to hold ribbing material which is not wound until after the body material has been applied.

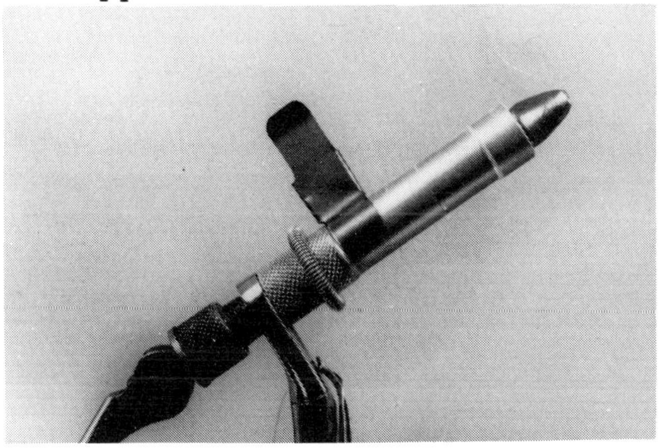

17

OPTIONAL TOOLS

Several optional tools may be used by the tier to facilitate the execution of his craft. Some of these are as follows:

A - RAZOR BLADE

A single-edge razor blade is small enough to remain out of the way on a tying table, and is handy to have available on certain infrequent occasions. Most cutting, of course, is done with your scissors, but should you want to strip practice materials from hooks, they are best removed with a razor blade. If you want to cut narrow strips from a flat piece of foam, leather, mylar or other such material, a razor blade often is preferable to your scissors. Just remember, a blade that is relatively new, and sharp, will be the safest to use.

B - FLAT NOSED PLIERS

These pliers have no serrations or teeth on their jaws. They serve two purposes in my tying procedures. First, they allow me to efficiently bend over the barb of the hook, as I prefer to fish with barbless hooks, and many hook styles are not available in the barbless form. Second, they can be used to great advantage in squeezing down the body of a fly when a flat profile is desired. The lead wire under the body material of a weighted flat-bodied nymph can be neatly flattened with this tool.

C - TWEEZERS

This modest tool is without question of more value to m'lady as she shapes the brows of her eyes, but the fly tier will find it useful mainly on two occasions. They work wonders in returning upright dry fly wings to an absolutely upright position should they happen to roll to the side while being secured to the hook shank. They are also of great benefit in holding the tip of a hackle feather as it is being dressed down prior to securing it to the hook. More on these procedures in their respective chapters.

D - HOOK HONE

Most hooks of a relatively small size are manufactured with extremely sharp points. Larger sized hooks, however, need to be examined, and a determination made as to whether they will penetrate the hard areas of a fish's mouth as efficiently as we'd prefer. My experience has shown that hooks of size #8 and larger usually should be touched up with the hook hone to give them a sharper point for easier penetration.

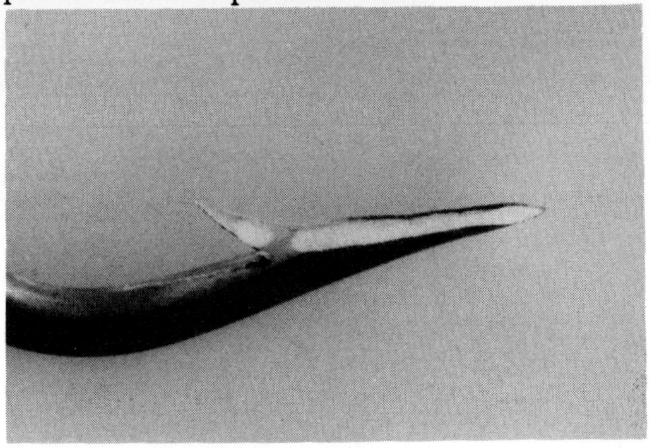

18

The standard method of sharpening the point is to create a triangular configuration by honing the bottom side of the point slightly flat, and creating the other two angles by honing the two sides of the point to create one cutting edge at the top and two cutting edges at the bottom of the hook point, PHOTO 18.

19

Several types of hones are available including solid Carborundum stone, serrated steel files, steel to which Carborundum stone has been affixed in a thin layer, and thin metal files to which diamond dust has been affixed, PHOTO 19. My personal preference is the solid piece of Carborundum stone pictured at the left in the photo. This type of hone is very efficient and should last for many years. It may break if dropped, so its fragile character must be respected.

E - BOBBIN REST

The type of bobbin rest described here is not, to my knowledge, available commercially. It's a homemade affair which need not be elaborate, but will definitely prevent aggravation which could otherwise occur. The rest shown in PHOTO 20 is in use. The rest is not being used in PHOTO 21 and the slow shutter speed shows the bobbin spinning.

20

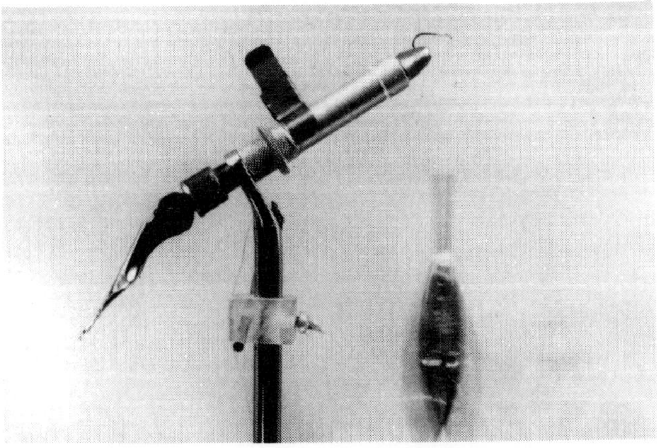

21

Between tying steps, the bobbin is placed on the rest to prevent it from spinning, which it usually wants to do if not placed on something stationary. The rests are nothing more than a bar of some type, attached to the vise so as to protrude toward the tier. One of the rests pictured is a nail taped to the vise stem. The other was made for me many years ago by a student who worked with plastics. A set screw holds the plastic block in place against the post. Another method, not shown, is to drill a hole through the post and insert a nail or piece of small metal tubing. These may then be simply taped in place to prevent them from sliding out of the hole.

I classify this device as an optional piece of equipment, but should you start using it, I don't think you'll want to be without it.

F - THREAD TWISTER

This can be a homemade device used in the application of some fur bodies and will be described in further detail in the chapter on bodies.

G - HAIR STACKER

As hair is cut from an animal skin, the tips of the hairs are not aligned as evenly as we require them to be when tying tails or wings. The hair stacker is a simple, but effective device to even the hair tips using a minimum of time and effort.

Most flies are made up of several component parts. For instance, the dry fly usually has a tail, body, wings and hackle. These components will be studied in detail throughout this book in their standard, time-proven methods of construction as well as more contemporary innovations developed in recent years.

The sequence of applying the various components to the hook shank varies from pattern to pattern, but generally for a standard wet fly the sequence is tail, body, hackle (legs) and wings. For a standard dry fly the sequence is wings, tail, body and hackle. I don't really consider the head of an artificial as a fly component, as it is a part of the structure which is present on 99% of our patterns, is repetitively tied in the same manner, in the same configuration, and with the same material (thread) on all our flies. Tying the head is the last step in our construction sequence.

I have structured the chapters of this book in a manner which will allow the novice to progress from the more simple procedures at first, to the more complex procedures later on. I strongly urge that each step along the way be mastered to a level of competency with which you are satisfied before you move along to the next step or the next chapter.

Good fly tiers, like good guitar players and good golfers, are made, not born; so the more you practice proper fundamentals, and the more you repeat the basics, the easier will be your transition to new techniques in the future.

With this introduction, we will now start to tie flies, not specific patterns, but all those elements which make up the completed fly.

SECURING THE THREAD TO THE HOOK

I ask you to pretend you're sitting at my side at the tying table. Our respective tools are in front of us, and our lamps are in position and directed on the jaws of the vise (which will be operated according to the manufacturer's instructions). For each procedure we cover, I will explain what we are doing, why we are doing it, and (via the photographs) show you how it's done. At that point, I want you to repeat the procedure I have explained. Then repeat it again, and maybe again, until you feel confident you can do it properly.

At the outset let me say this: it will be far better for your future proficiency at fly tying if you practice the procedures in this book with accuracy and care, rather than with a desire for immediate speed. I'm sure any accomplished tier can tell you that speed comes with practice, but in the long run, there's no substitute for tying the fly properly, even though at first it may be at a slow pace.

From this point forward throughout the book, you will be learning actual tying techniques in a step-by-step process. I want you to read each technique *completely through*, from first step to last, before you commence the physical execution of step number one. Reading through entirely will give you a general idea of what is expected of you and what final result you are to accomplish. Then go back to step one and perform it word by word.

A - INSERTING THE HOOK

Our first act will be that of inserting the hook into the jaws of the vise. Let's use a size #12 hook, Mustad #94840. The hook should be placed so that the shank is parallel with the table top. The point and barb are surrounded by the jaws so that no sharp points are protruding to catch and break the thread. The shank is positioned high enough to allow maximum room between it and the jaws. This room is necessary to facilitate the greatest ease in applying materials and winding the thread, PHOTO 22.

The space between the jaws, that space in which the hook is being grasped, will be positioned at a right angle to the surface of the table. If the vise is one which has a rotating sleeve, the jaws normally will be stationary in this 90 degree position, but the vise adjustment will allow the jaws to rotate while still firmly gripping the hook. This type of vise allows us to turn the hook upside down without removing it from the vise. The handle or knob of the vise should be tightened to a point where thread pressure, while tying, will not move the hook shank from the horizontal position.

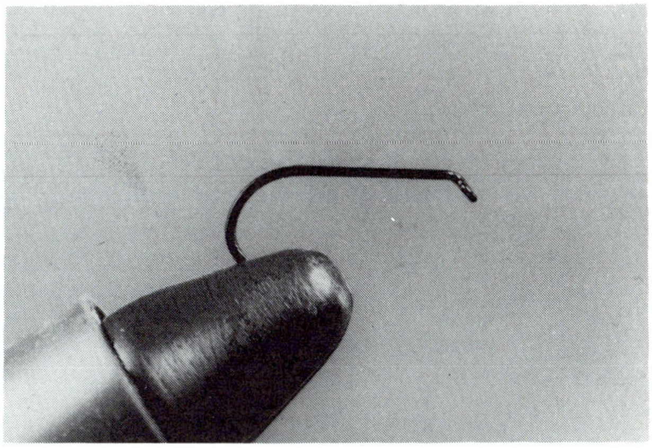

22

B - ATTACHING THE THREAD

The hook should now be directly out from the middle of our chest and at a height opposite our breast bone, which is approximately six to eight inches above the table top.

Attaching the thread to the shank will be the first step in tying all of our flies. With the bobbin in the right hand and about three inches of thread coming off the end of the tube, we hold the loose end of the thread in our left hand, between thumb and forefinger. Set the thread down on top of the shank with the bobbin on the far side of the hook and your left hand on the near side, PHOTO 23. Holding tension on the thread with both hands, wind the bobbin-thread around the shank by bringing the bobbin up toward your chin, then away from your face (clockwise when looking directly at the eye of the hook), with each successive turn laying to the *left* of the previous turn. You will now be covering the thread being held stationary with your left hand, PHOTO 24. Five or six turns will secure the thread, and permit you to release the bobbin allowing it to hang from the hook shank. The thread which you held with your left hand should now be clipped with your scissors as close to the shank as possible, PHOTO 25. Are you tying with your scissors held in your hand?

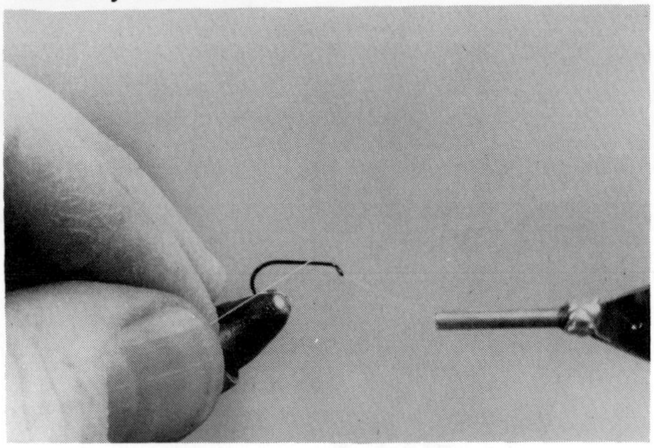

23

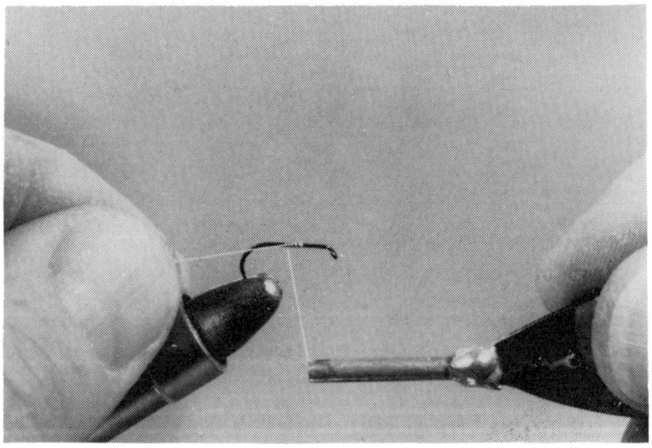

24

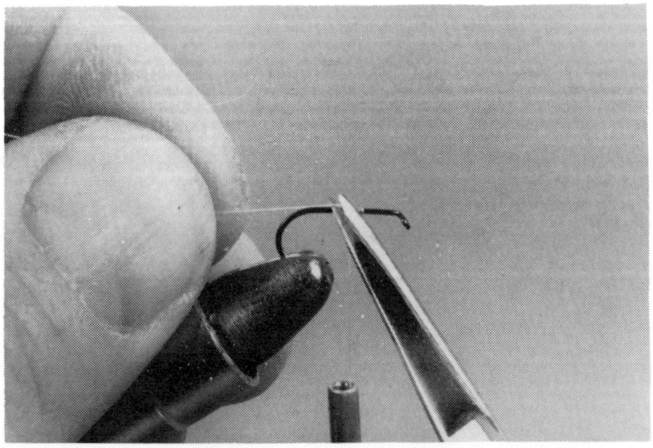

25

The foregoing paragraph has brought to light two basic "musts" of tying technique. The first is to *always keep tension on the thread.* This discipline is extremely important, as constant tension is a main factor in tying a durable fly. When thread tension is released, the materials under the winds may slip or move to a different position, or may actually become separated from the hook completely while the fly is being fished.

To stress the practical logic of this rule with an analogy, just recall the last time you wrapped a package with twine for mailing. Remember how you were always pulling on the twine to keep it tight? And when it came time to tie the knot, you asked someone to put his finger on the first overhand knot so the twine wouldn't loosen as you tied the balance of the knot. The same principle applies to fly tying thread. Keep it taut! A fly must not only be symmetric and properly proportioned, but it must also be durable!

The second basic "must" mentioned is to *cut away and discard those pieces of material which become excess and will not be required again on the fly.* Examples of such material include the stub of thread we just trimmed away, the butt or stub ends of feathers and hairs we tie to the shank to form wings and legs and tails and other fly parts, and lastly the tying thread itself when the fly is competed. Mention of this rule will be made several times throughout this book.

THE HALF HITCH KNOT

Now that we have the thread secured to the hook shank, our next exercise will be the tying of the half hitch knot. This knot will be the first of only two knots we need to master, but one we may not use in the dressing of many patterns. You'll rarely use the half hitch, but you must know how to tie it when certain infrequent situations require its use.

Some tiers recommend use of this knot after each step of the fly's construction. My experience has shown that when the turns of thread over material are tight, and if tension is never released, these knots are not necessary. The half hitch is necessary, however, when a subsequent procedure will require that tension be taken from the thread. These occasions are rare, but do exist. I don't want these remarks to be construed in any way as a criticism toward those tiers who advocate the use of the knot on all flies. My feeling is simply that it isn't necessary.

This is the procedure for its execution.

1. With the thread secured to the hook shank, hold the bobbin in your *left* hand, with approximately five inches of thread exposed with which to work. Place the index and middle fingers of your right hand down on top of the taut thread with about 1/4 inch space between them. Pinch the thread between thumb and index finger, PHOTO 26. Your middle finger should now be one inch from the hook.

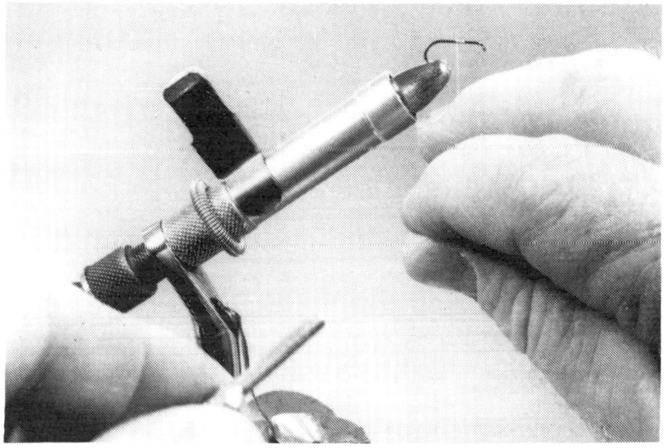

26

2. With thread still kept taut, roll the right hand away from you 90 degrees and allow the thread to lay across the *tip* of your index finger, PHOTO 27, *not* across the side of the finger, PHOTO 28. Next place the thread against the *backside* of the hook shank and hold it there with the index finger tip.

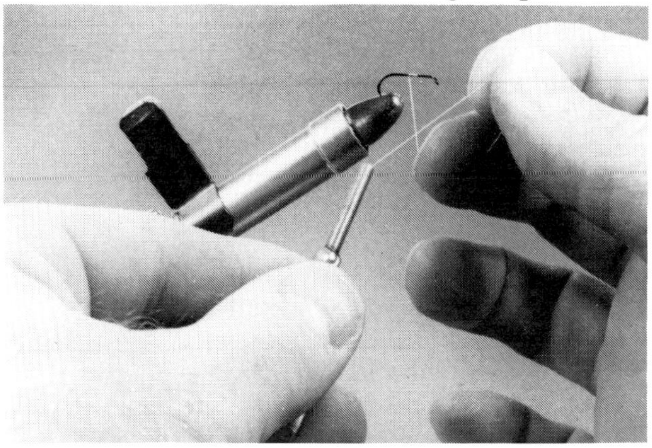

27

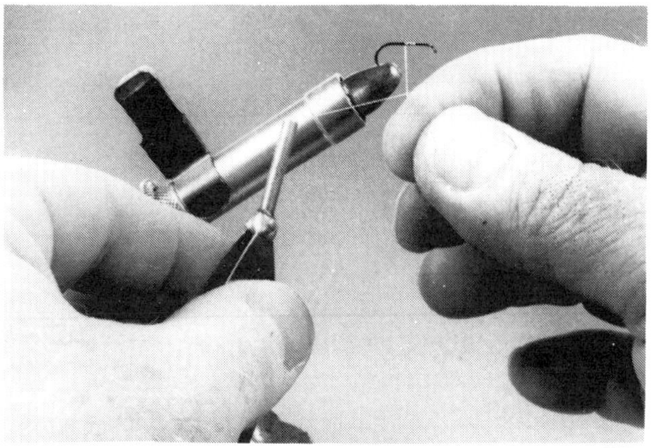

28

3. Remove the *middle finger only* from the loop of thread and pull the thread to your left with the bobbin to tighten the knot, PHOTO 29. That's it! You've tied the half hitch.

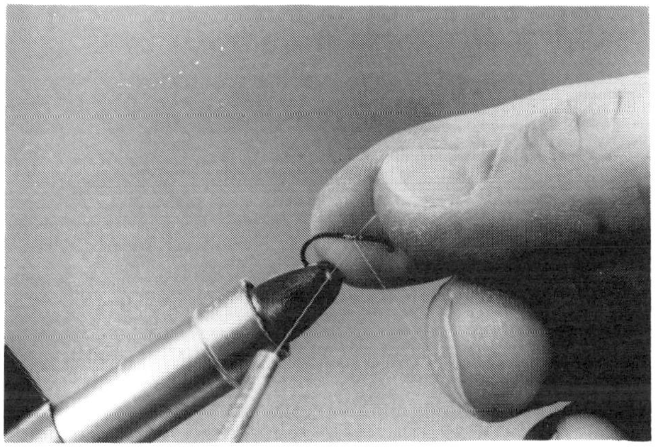

29

The tip of your index finger can position the thread wherever you wish behind the hook shank. Because this finger *stays in place* when pulling the knot tight, the knot will remain where you hold it.

It's important when pulling this knot tight, that you *do not remove your thumb* from the hook. It stays against your first finger to keep the tightening loop *under* the shank and prevents the loop from inadvertently tying down material on top of the hook. Try tying the knot holding only your first finger against the shank to visually understand this reasoning.

THE WHIP FINISH KNOT

This knot is the second, and last, knot we'll learn. It's used to finish off the dressing of each fly and is the last step in tying most flies. Its purpose is to assure that the head of the fly will not unravel and it can also be used to help build up the proper taper to the head.

The principle of the whip finish is to wind several turns of one part of the tying thread over a single strand of an adjacent part, and then pull these turns tight to create a firm bond of coils over the single strand.

This knot can be tied in three effective ways.

A - FIRST METHOD—WITH FINGERS ONLY

This method is performed similarly to the half-hitch, with the fingers only, but is an extension of the half-hitch knot procedure.

1. To execute this knot we assume the fly has been completely tied, and we are now ready to finish off the head. For this exercise, the thread is hanging slightly behind the eye of the hook. Pull the bobbin until six to eight inches of thread is exposed. With bobbin in the left hand, bring the index and middle fingers of the right hand up against the *left* side of the thread, with the inside of the fingers on the thread, PHOTO 30. Holding the thread taut, roll the right hand away from you until your palm is facing *up*, and put the resultant loop over the eye of the hook, PHOTO 31.

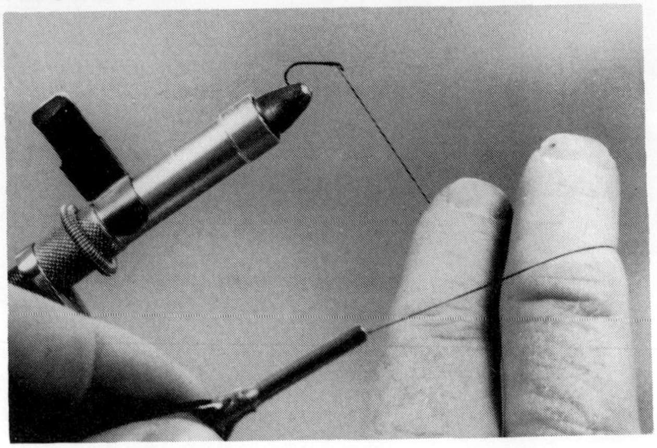

30

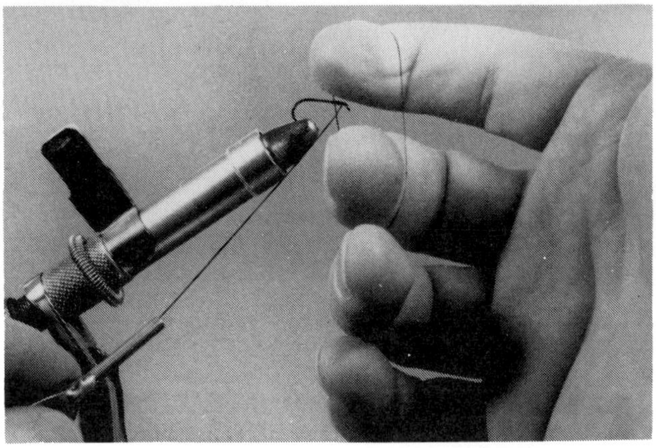

31

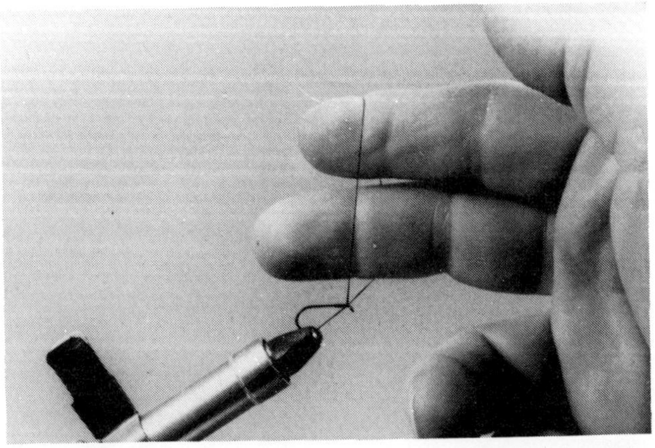

32

2. Now position these two fingers so they are in a vertical plane, with the middle finger below the index finger, PHOTO 32. Now

with all the thread taut, roll the thread loop away from you around the hook shank keeping the fingers one to two inches away from the shank until your fingers are under it, PHOTO 33. While executing this roll, keep the index finger above the middle finger. Twist your right hand far to the right so the index finger forces the near thread to change position and actually become the far thread, PHOTO 34.

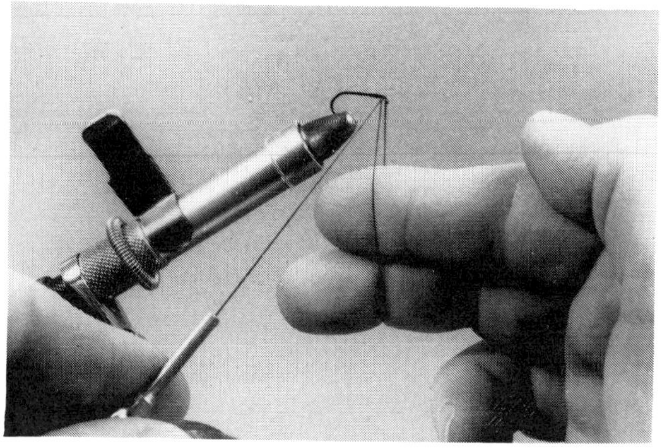

33

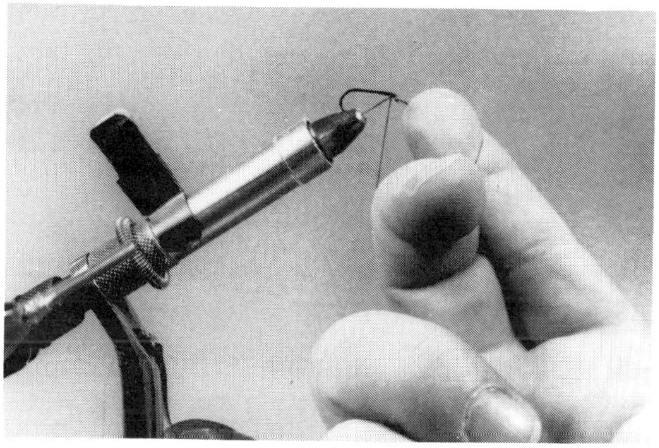

34

3. Now bring your fingers and the thread loop up above the shank, with the loop going over the eye, and again align your index and middle fingers in the vertical plane. Roll the fingers around to the under-the-hook position, PHOTO 33. You have now made the first coil of thread around the "bobbin thread," that which is coming from the tip of the bobbin tube.

4. Repeat steps two and three a total of four times, winding each successive coil to the left of the previous one and stopping the last roll with the fingers *under* the shank. By so doing, you will form a smooth and strong knot, and be in a position to perform the last step of the whip finish.

5. This next step completes the knot. From your present finger position under the shank, remove your index finger from the loop of thread. With it and your thumb, pinch the head of the fly to keep all thread coils in position. Then tighten the knot by pulling to your left with the bobbin, PHOTO 35, removing the middle finger when necessary. The knot is now complete and the bobbin thread should be cut as close to the head as possible. For this operation, use one blade of your scissors—just press the cutting edge against the thread.

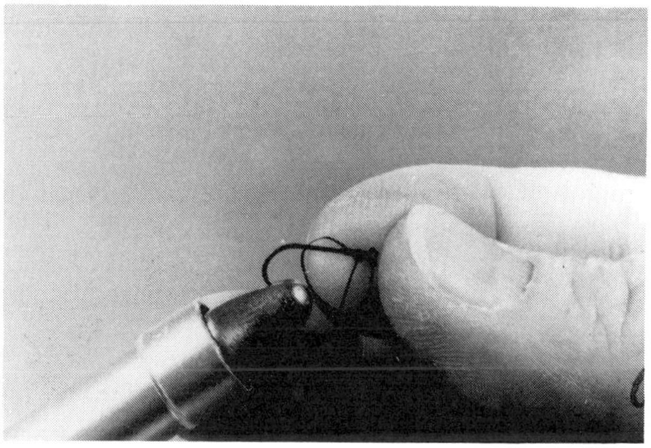

35

To completely finish the fly at this stage, you will coat the head of the fly with head cement, lacquer or varnish, using the point of your bodkin. Head cement is most commonly used.

B - SECOND METHOD—WITH MONOFILAMENT LOOP

This second method is performed with the help of a loop of small diameter nylon monofilamen. Thread or wire can also be used, but the mono performs very nicely.

The loop of mono is placed against the head of the fly using the left hand, PHOTO 36. With the bobbin in the right hand, four or five winds of thread are made around the loop and the hook shank, again with successive turns to the left of the previous turns, PHOTO 37. Next, place the tip of your left index finger on the head to hold the turns in place. Transfer the bobbin to your left hand and cut the bobbin thread leaving three inches of thread to work with in completing the knot. Push the thread through the mono loop, hold this thread taut with your right hand, PHOTO 38, and pull the mono loop to your left with your left hand until the thread end has been pulled underneath all the turns, PHOTO 39. Trim and cement as in Method A.

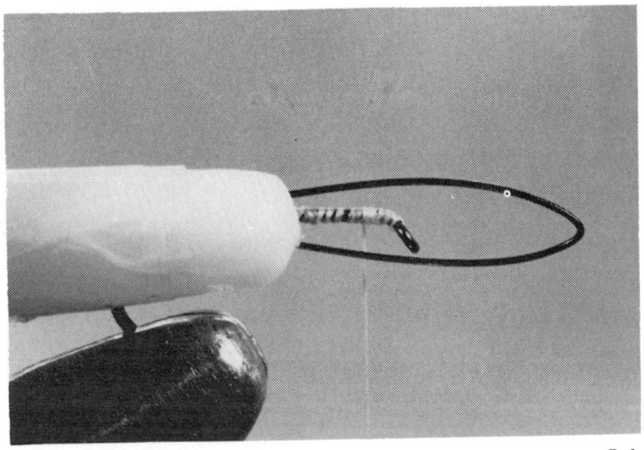

36

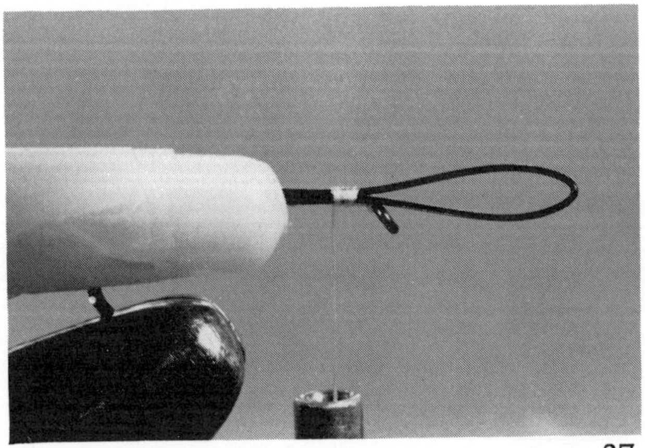

37

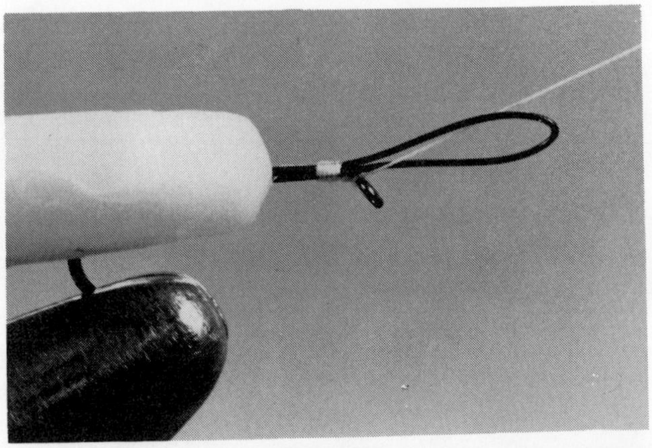

38

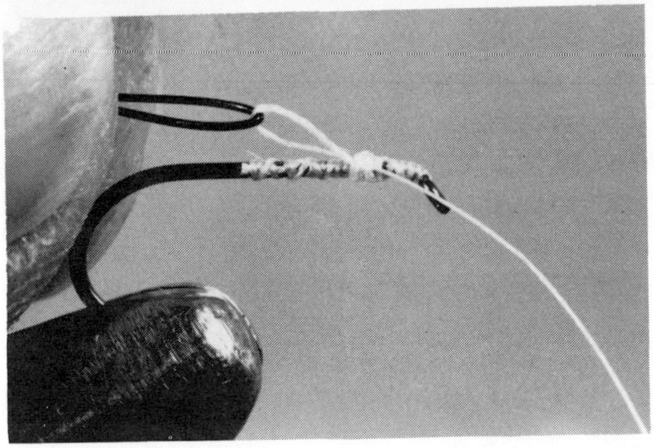

39

If you eventually prefer this method over the other methods of tying the whip finish knot, it's a good idea to wind or tape the monofilament to a handle of some sort for convenience (as in the photos).

In all these methods it is essential to keep the thread *taut* to assure the tightest knot possible.

C - THIRD METHOD—WITH THE WHIP FINISH TOOL

The whip finishing tool is used here, and in my judgment this method is the quickest and easiest method for tying the whip finish knot. The tool is not difficult to use, but it is tricky when first practiced, and certain elements of the procedure must be done properly to avoid frustration.

The whip finisher consists of a knurled handle, a "U"-shaped spring with a hook on one end (A), a coil (D) on the other, and the point of the tool with two hooks at its tip (B & C), PHOTO 40a.

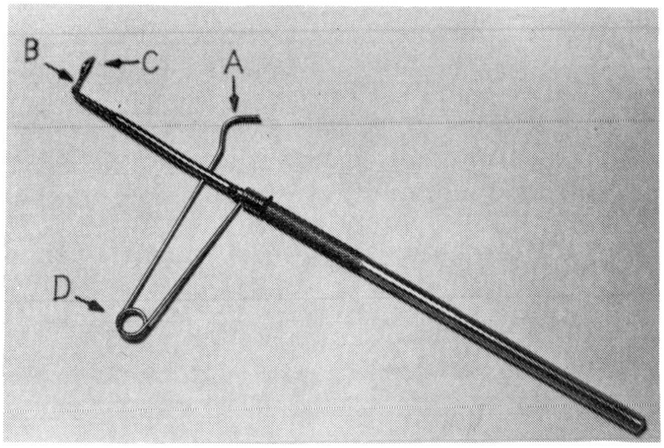

40a

The step-by-step procedure is as follows:

1. Attach the thread to a hook. With the bobbin in the left hand, pull out about five inches of thread.

2. The end of the tool shaft is held against the palm of the hand with the little and ring fingers, PHOTO 40b. With the tool properly held in the right hand, with the spring coil (D) in a down position, set the thread into hook A and without moving the tool, move the bobbin thread to your left and set it into hook B, PHOTO 41.

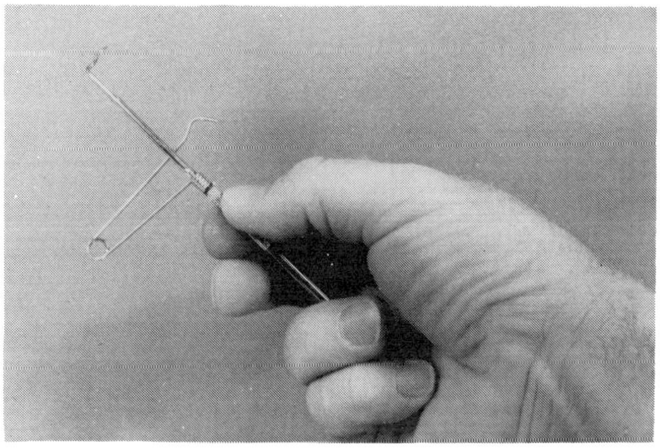

40b

3. Now slowly *rotate* the tool between your thumb and index finger 180 degrees until the coil (D) is in an upright position. Stop here. As this rotation is accomplished, the *only* movement of the left hand is to raise the bobbin thread *slightly*, PHOTO 42. This subtle lift of the thread will prevent it from falling out of hook B. Don't neglect to make this simple move!

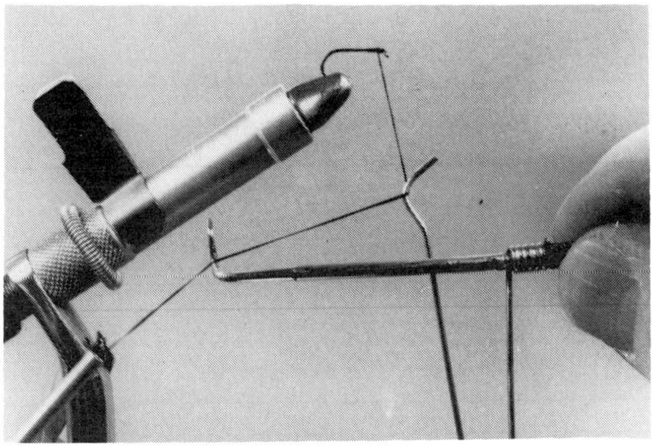

41

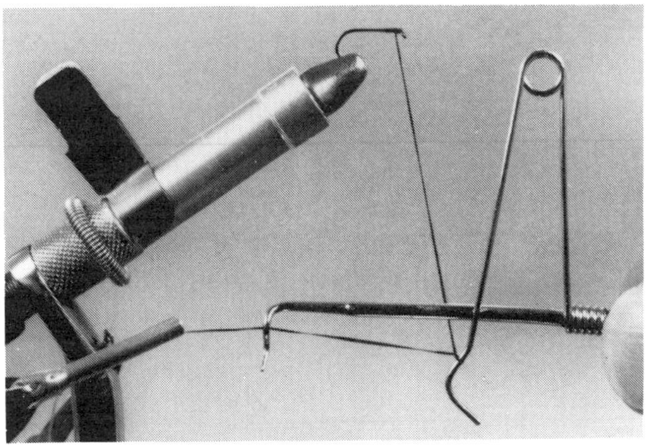

42

4. With hook C, come up over the thread coming off the shank and catch it on the *far* side allowing this thread to rest in the bend of hook C, PHOTO 43.

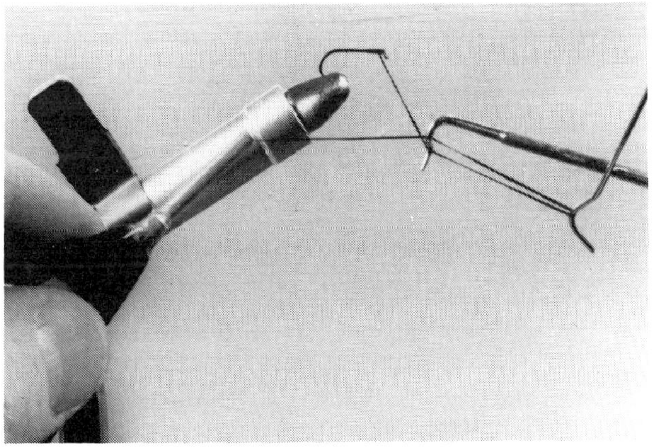

43

5. Now, keeping all of the thread taut, slide the tool up to the shank, rest the bend of hook B against the head of the fly and hold the tool handle straight out from, and in alignment with, the hook shank, PHOTO 44.

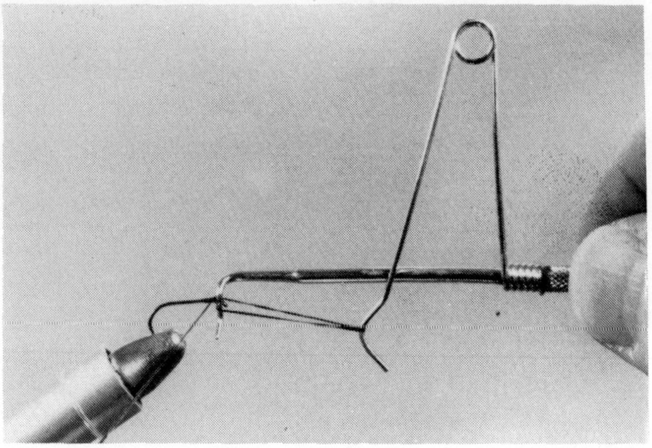

44

6. This next step should be done *slowly* and with deliberate care. Speed is not important as you learn this procedure, but will come easily with practice. We now *rotate* the tool around the fly head, but always maintaining contact between the fly head and the tool (at hook B). The natural tendency by beginners is to *roll* the tool, thereby losing this essential contact between head and hook B resulting in a "lost" knot. Contact is essential! *Rotate* the tool carefully, always pressing the tool against the head. Four or five rotations should be made and then the tool should be stopped with the spring coil *up*, PHOTO 44.

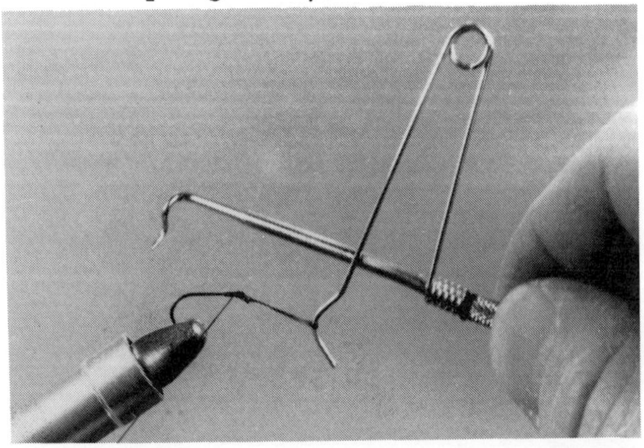

45

7. This last step is simple. Disengage the entire point of the tool from the fly head and pull the thread to your left with the bobbin, PHOTO 45. This pulling tightens and completes the knot.

Practice this entire procedure slowly about 20 times. You should then be accomplishing the technique with relative ease and noticeably increased speed.

8. **Helpful Hints**

In using this tool, a few observations should be noted.

a. Don't allow the left hand to wander. It remains essentially stationary, comfortably in front of you, and does only three things: it sets the thread into hook B in step two; it lifts the thread slightly in step three; and it pulls the knot tight in step seven.

b. The tool should be rotated as if the handle was stuck into the wall. In other words, it rotates in a *stationary* position. Your right hand does *not* move up and down, round and round, or back and forth during this procedure. It remains basically fixed in one position.

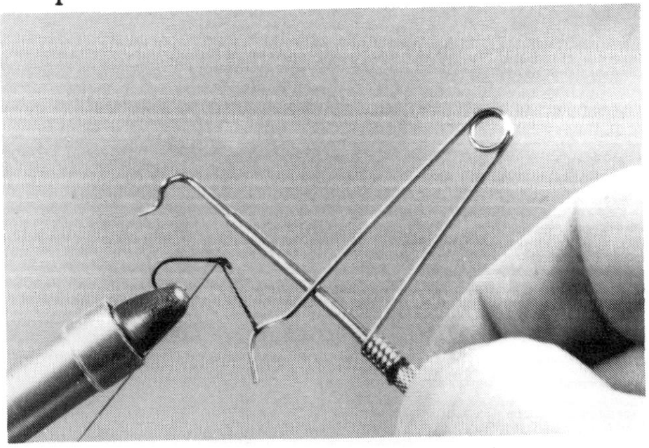

46

c. Just before pulling the knot tight in step seven, move your right hand, and the tool, slightly toward your chest so that the threads are not positioned directly out over the hook eye, but rather are coming off the near *side* of the head, PHOTO 46. This simple act will prevent the threads from possibly catching the sharp edge on the end of the wire which was bent to form the eye. Nothing can be more frustrating than cutting or fraying your thread while performing this last step of tying the fly.

d. A last tip is required here to assist you in solving a particular problem which may arise when you are finishing the head of a large fly, like a streamer, or if you merely get carried away and make too many winds of thread around the head. The problem is that of loading the spring too tightly. In other words, during the process of rotating the tool, the hook (A) is pulled up too close to the tip hooks (B & C). Many times in this situation the knot will explode and fall apart when you try to slip the thread off hook C immediately prior to pulling the knot tight.

The method of relieving the overload on the spring is as follows: with the first finger of the right hand merely reach forward in front of the extended arm of the spring, PHOTO 47a, and pull it back to a less loaded position, PHOTO 47b. Now you can either continue to make more turns of the tool, or you can slip hook C away from the fly and tighten the knot.

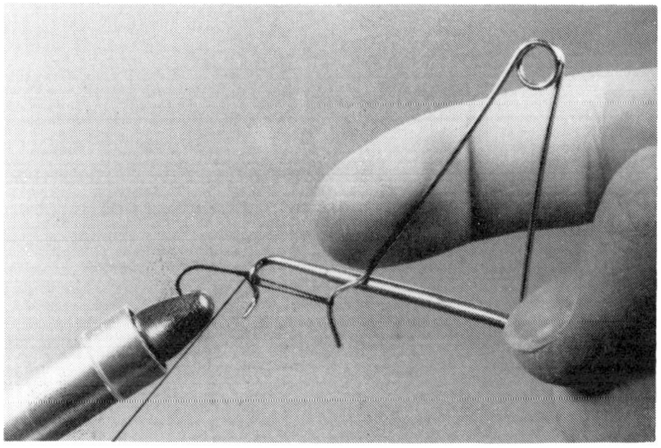

47a

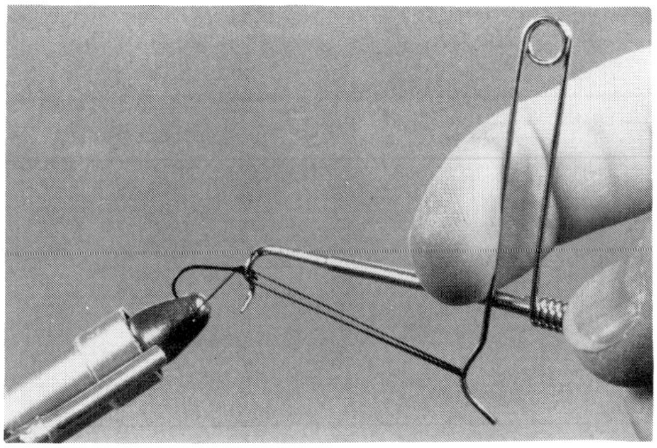

47b

Now you know how to tie the knots of fly tying. If you have practiced each of them several times, I trust you found they are not really difficult to perform. And if you will follow the other procedures outlined in this book with patience and practice, I think you'll find the tying of complete flies is not difficult to perform.

The tail of an artificial fly accomplishes two main functions. In almost all cases it represents the actual tail of the insect we are imitating and, in the case of a dry fly, it is tied also to assist the fly in floating on the water's surface. Dry fly tails are generally tied of a material which is relatively stiff to prevent the tail from "collapsing" and sinking when it lands on the water. Another favorable characteristic of dry fly tails is that they be of a material which is not water absorbant. Materials which absorb water readily will obviously sink faster than those which remain dry. The material should have a low specific gravity. In other words, it should weigh less than water, and therefore tend to float well. A tail of lead wire might be stiff and would be non-water absorbant, but certainly would have no inclination to float due to its high specific gravity.

Another desirable feature of tailing material is translucency, the characteristic allowing light to pass through it. The advantage of this feature is that it is more life-like because most parts of an insect allow some light to pass through.

The tails of wet flies should also be translucent, but the features of stiffness, non-absorbancy and low specific gravity are not important because we want the fly to sink immediately upon contact with the water. However, in the case of both types of flies, the materials should be supple enough to move and bend with the water currents just as the tails of most actual insects.

We usually try to use those materials which possess as many of the above qualities as possible for the type of fly we are tying, but sometimes we sacrifice one feature to gain the advantage of another. Our minds must remain open and flexible, and not adverse to experimentation or change, as may be dictated by need or personal inclination.

Materials used for tailing the artificial fly fall into basically two categories: those for dry flies and those for wet flies. The most commonly used material for dry fly tails is the fibers (sometimes called wisps or barbules) from the feather of a dry-fly quality hackle neck. These fibers seem to possess all the characteristics essential for imitating the tail of an adult insect floating on the water. They are delicate, stiff, water repellent and float well under most conditions, particularly when treated with a good silicone fly dressing.

In tying flies which we expect to use in rough-water conditions where the fly is susceptible to being pulled under or dunked by a choppy water surface, tails tied of animal hair are used extensively. The most common hair used is that from the body of a deer. This hair, as well as that from the body of an elk or caribou, has the desirable characteristic of being hollow. When a clump of these fibers is secured to the hook shank, it's not difficult to imagine how well it will float on the water.

You will use many other hairs and fibers throughout your fly tying experience, but I don't intend to discuss all of them here. What we intend to learn now is the method by which general types of materials will be attached to the hook. It's not my intention to explain in minute detail all the knowledge gained from my personal experience of trial and error with many different materials. That's a privilege which you should enjoy on your own. There are many fields of endeavor which hold anticipation, mystery, and challenge which can be best learned, evaluated, and enjoyed through self-discovery. I don't wish to deprive you of those pleasures. My goal is, however, to relay the fundamental means by which you can make these realizations on your own.

The following general rules concerning tails are listed as being important for standard dry flies. This listing will lay a procedural groundwork which will be followed on most of the dry flies you tie. These ground rules are listed here for reference, and they will also be explained in more detail when we start the step-by-step trying procedures.

1. **Tail fibers should be two gaps long.**

A tail which is too short and stubby will not give adequate floating support to the fly. The weight of the steel hook would pull it under the water's surface. A tail which is too long, on the other hand, would tend to bend and collapse excessively and also not give the fly adequate floating properties. In both cases, the fly would also look unnatural and out of proportion with its other parts. The two-gap length, from the tips of the fibers to the point where it is secured to the hook shank, offers both good balance and proportion, plus a proper floating characteristic. PHOTO 53 illustrates a good dry fly tail.

2. **Use approximately twelve fibers.**

This quantity refers to the number of individual hackle fibers. Again a judgment factor must be exercised to determine the quantity used, and a dozen offers good flotation without being too bulky. In the case of *hair* tails, about two dozen fibers work well, as the fly is not tied to be a delicate representation, but rather is tied to float well under rough-water conditions.

3. **Set the fibers on a base of thread.**

One of our basic goals in fly tying is to tie a pattern which is durable. We don't want materials changing position on the shank or falling out as the fly is fished. The rule here prevents both problems. The metal hook is smooth and therefore slippery. If the fibers are set onto the bare metal and then bound down with winds of thread, there's a good possibility the fibers will roll around the shank into an unwanted position. Setting them on a waxed thread base prevents this possibility.

4. **Tie in fibers on top of the hook shank.**

This rule simply means that the fibers should not be allowed to roll around the hook shank to a position on the side of, or underneath, the shank. Such poor positioning would tend to unbalance the fly, and possibly make it sit poorly on the water.

5. **Tie fibers straight out from the shank.**

The tail should not droop, nor should it bend upwards. Either situation will make the fly float improperly. In the case of a wet fly or nymph, this rule isn't as critical because the material used is normally softer and will be moved by the water currents. The fibers of the dry fly, however, should look like an extension of the hook shank itself.

6. **Flare the fibers slightly.**

For purposes of delicacy, and increased floatability, the fibers should not all be lumped together. Rather, they should be separated into a slight flare with a very small space between all the fiber tips. Ideally, this flare would result in the tips forming a circle when viewed directly from the rear of the fly. This circle would facilitate the fly's rolling over to an upright position should it land upside-down on the water when cast; much more so, obviously, than if the fibers were all lying in a flat plane. The flare also puts more fibers into contact with the water's surface film, and thus promotes a better floating capability.

48

7. **Use no webby material on the fibers.**

Following this listing of general rules, we will actually tie a tail to the hook. Our first tail will be of hackle fibers (barbules) as shown in PHOTO 48. In looking closely at the photo, you will notice the fibers contain a darker portion close to the quill (stem) of the feather. The denser portion is known as web and derives its name from the fact that it consists of very tiny fibers emerging from each long fiber. The web is soft and water absorbant, and therefore not desirable for use on a dry fly. It is, however, used extensively on wet flies for these same two reasons.

On most, but not all, hackle feathers the web can be seen easily with a little practice. A more dramatic realization of its existence can be gained by looking at a feather through a magnifying glass. To avoid utilizing web in our tails, we must select a feather large enough to supply fibers from which we will have a tail two gaps long, with no web showing in the tail itself.

8. **Never cut the tips from tail fibers to shorten them.**

The tail should always be tied in at the proper length to begin with, rather than trimming the fibers to shorten the tail to a proper length.

With these basic rules in mind, let's proceed to the tying of our first dry fly tail.

THE HACKLE FIBER TAIL

1. Insert a size 12 dry fly hook (#94840) into the jaws of your vise.

2. Attach the thread to the hook as learned in the chapter on knots.

3. Wind the thread back to the point immediately in front of the start of the bend. Now wind thread 1/8 inch to your right. This is your base thread. Allow the bobbin to hang at this point, or lay it over your bobbin rest.

4. Dress down a large hackle feather you have selected from a dry-fly quality neck. To

dress the feather down, hold the tip in your left hand in a vertical position, and pull the fibers down toward the butt of the quill with your right hand, PHOTO 48. You may have to dress down two or three times to make the fibers stand out relatively perpendicular to the quill. (For more information on the neck itself see Chapter Six on Hackles.)

5. Now dress down enough so that at least a dozen long fibers are exposed on the *left* side of the quill. Stop dressing and continue to pinch the feather with the right hand. With the feather still held in a vertical position, grasp these dozen or so fibers with the left thumb and index finger by pinching them together vertically, PHOTO 49.

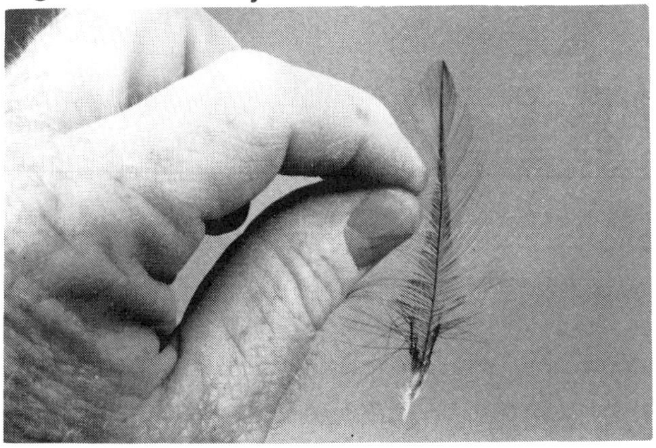

49

6. Now release the feather with the right hand. Re-grasp the tip of the feather with the right hand, continue to hold the fibers in the left hand firmly, and snap your hands apart. The tail fibers are now gripped in your left fingers ready to tie onto the shank.

7. The feather from which you took the fibers may be set aside and used for other tails. Usually two tails can be taken from each side of a feather, for a total of four flies.

Now grasp the bobbin in the right hand, with three to four inches of exposed thread between the hook and the bobbin tube. Hold the fibers about 1/16 to 1/8 inch *above* the shank of the hook with your left hand as in PHOTO 50.

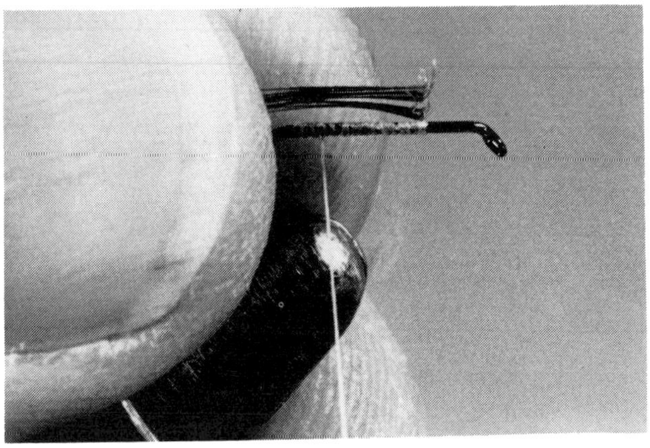

50

8. With thread taut, bring the bobbin toward you and raise the thread to a vertical position, slightly pinching the thread between thumb and index finger of the left hand, PHOTO 51. With the thread thus pinched, you may release the tension on the bobbin thread as you wind completely around the fibers and shank. Again pinch the thread after you've wound to the vertical position. Still pinching the fibers, the shank and the turns of thread with the left hand, lift the bobbin straight up. This movement will tighten the coils of thread around the fibers; holding them on top of, and firmly against, the hook shank. *Do not* release tension on the thread.

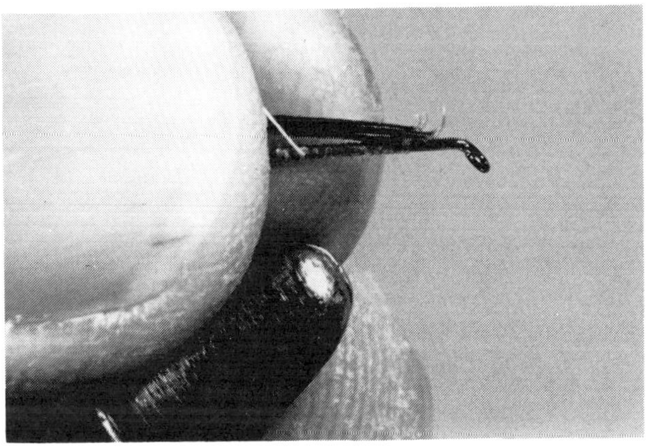

51

9. You may now remove the left hand and view your work. Re-grasp the fibers slightly to the left of where you previously held them,

PHOTO 52, and wind the thread to your left until you have wound far enough to cover the winds of the base thread. You do not want the base thread to be visible under the tail!

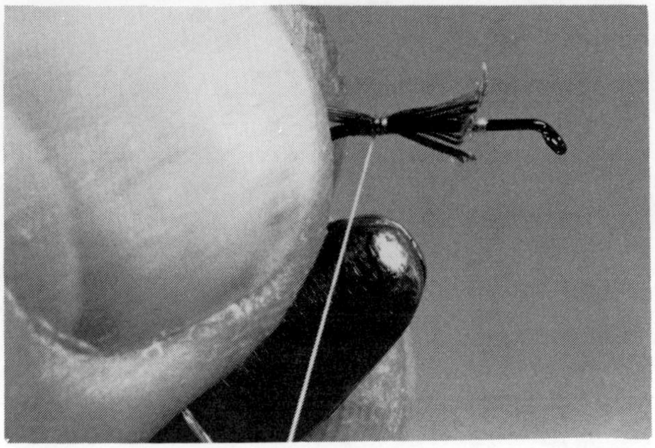

52

As these turns of thread are being made over the fibers, continue to hold the fibers with the left hand to assure they remain on *top* of the shank. It takes approximately *six winds of thread* to properly secure material of any kind. Remember, we want the fly to be durable! The fibers should be two gaps long and on top of the shank, PHOTO 53. At this stage, cut away the butts of hackle fiber extending to the right of the tie-down. You'll notice that if you continue to wind to the left down the bend of the hook, the tail will follow the bend, and start to droop. This is a condition you must avoid on dry flies!

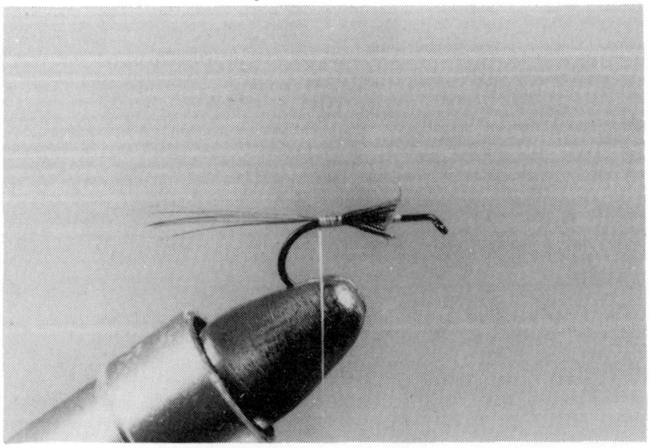

53

Your tail is now tied in, but we have one other feature to look for: the flare of the fibers. Ninety-five percent of the time the tail will flare naturally as it is tied, but in the event it doesn't, here is the way to make it do so. Merely make one more wind of thread, but this time wind it *under* the tail fibers rather than over them. In other words, the thread goes between the fibers and the hook shank, PHOTO 54. After you have passed the thread under the tail, give it a slight tug forward (toward the hook eye). This pressure under the fibers should flare them slightly and you need only make a couple more winds over your original tie-down winds to assure the under-the-tail wind doesn't lose its tension.

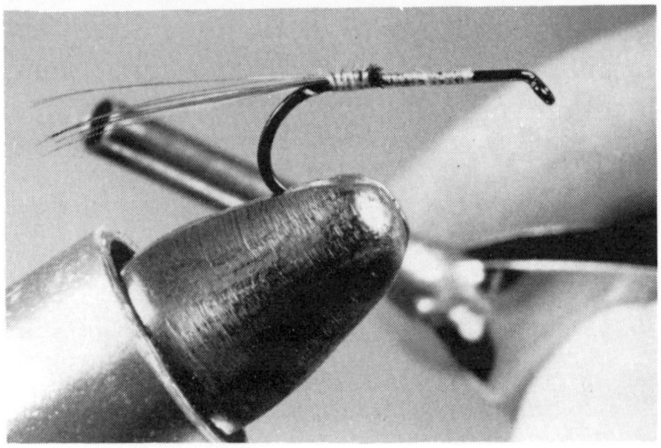

54

That's it! You have now tied a tail which is not only durable, but it looks great and will give good support to your fly as it floats on the water.

Now that we actually have a part of the fly tied down to the hook shank, this is a proper time to teach you to fix an occasional problem that bedevils all tiers. Every now and then, for one reason or another, our thread breaks. We have materials attached to the hook and all of a sudden our thread is hanging limply from the shank with no tension to keep these materials in place and no connection to the bobbin to allow progress to the next step.

Don't panic! A minor repair is all that's necessary and you'll accomplish it with no trouble at all. The first thing to do, using the jaws of your hackle pliers, is grasp the loose thread protruding from the fly and allow the pliers to hang freely from the shank. This will provide thread tension and control. Now re-thread the bobbin if necessary, and attach the thread to the hook as if you were starting to tie a new fly. Wind the bobbin thread over the broken stub to secure it in place, PHOTO 55, cut away the two stub threads, and you are now ready to proceed with the next regular tying step.

55

Thread breakage can usually be attributed to applying too much pressure to it; it has caught on a hook point which was not buried completely into the jaws of the vise; it's been cut by the sharp edge of a strip of tinsel; it's been snagged on the wire-end at the eye of the hook; or possibly it was cut when rubbed against a sharp leading edge of the vise jaws. No matter what the reason, the remedy is not difficult.

THE HAIR TAIL

The procedures for tying hair (usually deer or elk body hair) is essentially the same as for the hackle fiber tail. There are a few differences however, and you'll learn them now. Read through all eight steps of this section before actually tying this tail.

1. Use a durable nylon thread for hair work.

2. You'll use approximately two dozen deer hairs, as opposed to the one dozen hackle fibers in the previous tail.

3. The hairs will be cut from the hide with scissors, as close to the hide as is practical. There will most likely be small fibers of under-fur mixed in with the hair. The majority of these should be pulled out with your fingers or can be removed with a fine-toothed pocket comb. This step will reduce the amount of bulk you will have to secure to the hook.

4. Because the *tip* ends of the hairs are not even, or flush with each other, you must even them manually after cutting them from the hide. One method is to hold the clump of fibers between the thumb and index finger of the right hand. I like to allow the clump to rest in the first knuckle crease of the finger. While holding the bundle *loosely* with the hair tips pointing to he left, tap the tips with the palm of the left hand, and allow the hairs to slide between the fingers and thumb, PHOTO 56. The longest fibers will slide first and each succeeding hair will even up with the others until all tips are flush with each other.

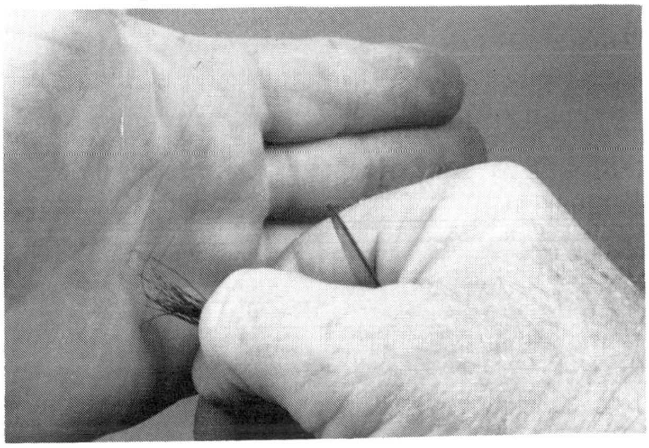

56

Another method would require the hairs be inserted tip first into a receptacle similar to a bullet casing. When the casing is tapped on the table, the hairs will settle, and automatically even themselves in the bottom of the case. When removed, they would be ready to hold in proper position to tie to the hook shank. There are hair stackers available commercially which do the same job with considerable ease.

5. Although we tie this tail onto a base of waxed thread, it's also a good idea to apply a small drop of head cement to the base thread just before setting the deer hair onto the hook. Hollow hair such as we are using, tends to roll easily around the shank, not only as we tie it in, but also after the fly has been mouthed by a fish or two. The cement helps to keep it in place.

6. As you wind your thread around one end of this bundle, and compress the hollow fibers, the reaction to this compression is an expansion at the opposite end. Hollow hair flares out exasperatingly until we learn to control it. Our method for doing so is really very logical, and not difficult.

57

With hollow hair tails, start your winds about 1/8 inch *forward* of where you did with the hackle fibers, or about 1/4 inch forward of the start of the bend. Tie in the hair as you did the hackle fibers by making several tight turns of thread. Allow the hair to flare at will, but keep it on *top* of the shank, PHOTO 57.

7. Now, as you continue to wind to your left, make several more winds relatively loosely. These looser turns will not compress the hair and will therefore bring the tips back close together, PHOTO 58. The thread now has covered the base thread and you are ready to tie the body.

58

With the above exceptions, the procedure and thread manipulation is identical to our hackle fiber tail. With each of these materials your tails should possess the general features listed early in this chapter.

OTHER TYPES OF TAILS

A - THE SPLIT TAIL—USING SEVERAL FIBERS

Insect tails do not extend from their abdomens in a single bundle. They protrude as two or three single, but separated, fibers. These tiny filaments serve their purpose in the anatomy of the insect, but certainly wouldn't help much in supporting the insect on the water were he attached to a steel hook. That's why we normally use more than two or three fibers on our artificials, for support!

However, we can imitate a more life-like appearance, and at the same time attain a more stable floating capability, by merely dividing our one fiber or hair bundle into two bundles. The procedure is relatively simple, but should be practiced a few times until it can be done easily. It goes like this:

1. Tie in a hackle fiber tail as previously described.

2. With your scissor points divide the tail into two equal bundles and hold the bundle nearest you with the thumb and index finger of the left hand. Pull the bundle toward you, PHOTO 59. Now bring the thread up over the top of this near bundle and then under the far bundle as you go around the hook for the first wind. You have now wedged thread between the bundles with the effect of separating them, PHOTO 60.

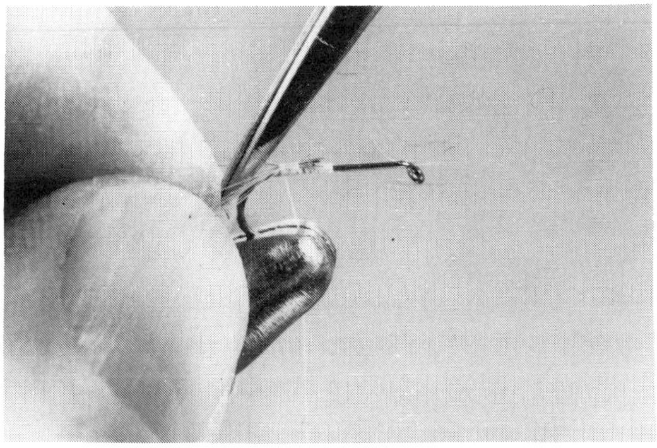

59

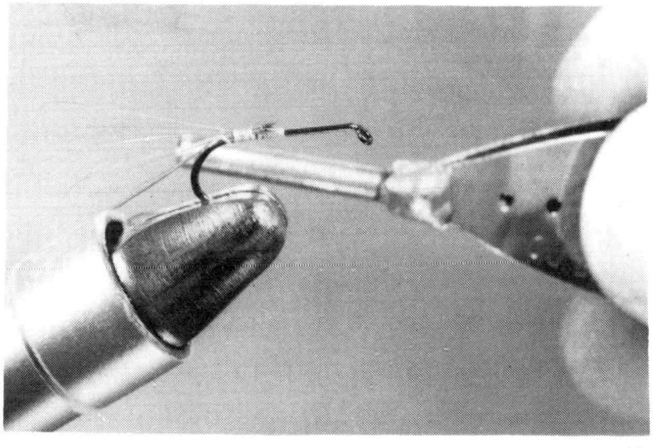

60

3. Make another wind of thread between the bundles, but this time come up *under* the near bundle and *over* the far bundle as you complete the wind. By executing steps two and three, you have completed what is known as a "figure 8." This figure 8 technique is merely a thread manipulation and is used often when dividing one group of material into two parts. You will use it very often when tying wings.

4. Continue making the figure 8's until the fibers are set into the position you desire, typically as in PHOTO 61. If needed, you may also take a wind or two of thread between the shank and the tails to lift them up if the figure 8's have bent them down.

61

B - THE SPLIT TAIL—USING ONLY TWO FIBERS

The bundle type tail which you have just learned obviously serves the purpose of floating the fly more than it serves the purpose of accurate insect tail imitation. This is particularly true in the case of a dry fly because the tail fibers of the natural insect are single filaments spread apart at angles from 45 to 75 degrees.

I know of no way to effectively tie the artificial tail in a manner which will present the very delicate appearance of the natural and at the same time provide the type of buoyancy required of it when fishing fast, rough water. We must, therefore, use a tying judgment which will produce the proper dressing for each of the different circumstances we encounter.

Tails for flies to be used on relatively calm, flat water can logically be tied in a manner which will present a more life-like appearance to the fish. Such a tail will consist of two or four fibers, equally divided and angled away from each other to give the "V" appearance of the natural. The instructions and illustrations for this exercise will demonstrate this tail using only two fibers.

When selecting the feather, fiber or animal hair to be used on this tail, it is important to select those fibers which are not brittle. Deer and elk hair, for example, tend to break easily, and therefore are not recommended for use singly. Other hairs are less brittle, and I find moose body, squirrel tail, mink tail, and polar bear hair to be extremely forgiving to rough treatment. Hackle fibers also work very well. They are softer and more flexible than the hairs, and therefore do not float as well, but they are more delicate and probably make better representations of the real thing than do the coarser animal hairs.

I'll let you do your own experimenting with different materials so you may make your own evaluations and establish your own preferences.

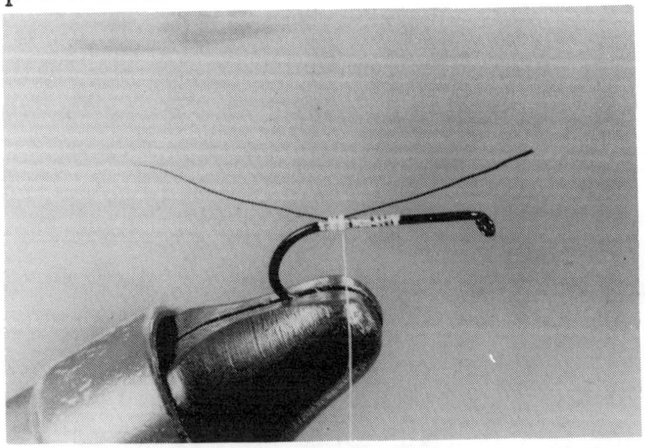

62

The two-fiber tail is tied as follows:

1. In the photos, I've used moose body hairs. On a base of thread, position one hair at approximately a 30 degree angle to the side from the shank, and wind five or six turns of thread over it to hold it in place. I prefer to tie in the far-side fiber first, PHOTO 62.

2. Now place the second fiber over the base thread at the same, but opposite, angle. Secure it with five or six winds. The fibers should now be the same length, and set at equal angles from the shank to give a symmetric and balanced appearance, PHOTO 63.

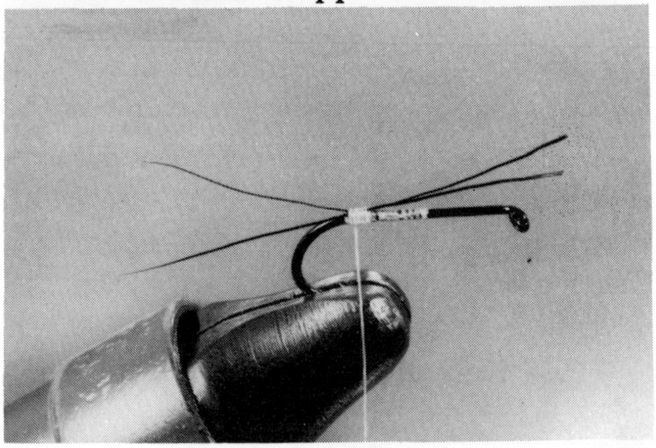

63

3. To assure this tail will retain its present position throughout the life of the fly, you may now figure 8 around each fiber. The thread wedged between the hairs and the shank will keep them properly positioned. You may also apply a small drop of cement over the tie-down thread to assure the tail doesn't change position.

For dry flies, I recommend tails of this type be tied on 3-extra fine wire hooks and in conjunction with body materials which have a high degree of floatability. It's obvious when looking at this tail, that the steel of the hook is going to exert considerable influence to pull the tail down through the water's surface. We need all the help we can get to keep it afloat!

Another material which works very well for the two-fiber tail is the bare *quill* of a hackle feather. We merely strip the fibers from the quill up as close to the tip of the feather as possible. For practical purposes this may be within 1/4 inch of the tip. The quill can then be cut at an angle with a razor blade to dispose of the few remaining fibers, and to put as much of a point on the quill as possible. Insect tails are not blunt on the ends, so neither should be our artificials. Cutting the quill with scissors at a 90 degree angle will create a blunt-ended tail.

C - THE SPLIT TAIL WITH FOUR FIBERS ON THE QUILL

This variation of the hackle fiber tail utilizes a small segment of the hackle quill itself, which we tie down on the shank. Our technique here is to select a hackle feather of the appropriate size to provide fibers of a *total* length equal to the length of tail we desire (usually two gaps long). We will not have the butt ends of the fibers to trim off as we have had in the past. Here's the procedure:

1. Dress the feather down.

2. At the point on the quill at which the total fiber length is the length you desire the tail to be, strip away the fibers toward the butt for a distance of about one inch. The first two remaining fibers emerging from each side of the quill should be emerging directly across from each other, PHOTO 64.

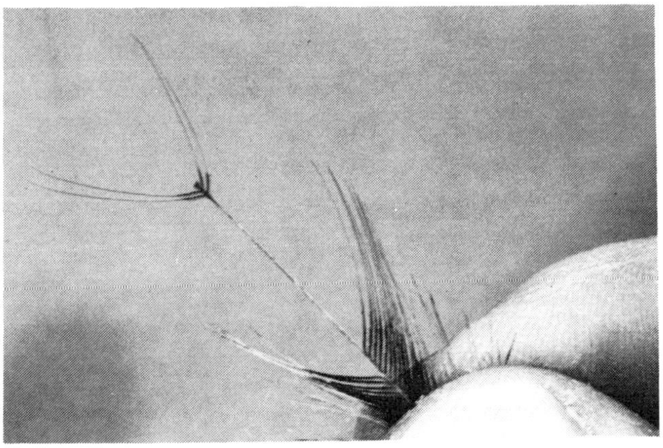

64

3. Because we want only two fibers remaining on each side of the quill, snip the quill with your scissor points immediately in front of the second pair of fibers coming from each side of the quill, PHOTO 64.

4. Now cut the quill again, 1/4 inch below the two pairs of fibers. This section of bare quill will be pinched flat with pliers or tweezers to help prevent it from rolling on the shank as it is tied in.

5. Set this flattened bare quill on your base thread and cinch it down with five or six turns of thread. The quill will be so positioned as to permit the dull (concave) side of the fibers to be on top, thus flaring upward and outward, PHOTO 65, as is typical of the living insect. For added security, apply a tiny drop of cement to the tie-down.

65

This type of tail is not restricted to fibers from a hackle neck, though they seem to be most effective for dry flies. The identical procedure can be used in tying wet fly tails but, rather than the hackle feather being used, the body feathers of many birds can be utilized as long as the feathers are of a size small enough to produce a tail of the proper length. These body feathers are soft and water absorbant and therefore well suited to wet fly application.

D - THE KEEL TAIL

This is a rarely used tail in the total spectrum of fly tying, but it is used on one extremely popular pattern and therefore worthy of our consideration. The pattern is the Muddler Minnow, used by many anglers throughout the country, particularly in the Western states.

The material originally used here was brown, mottled turkey wing quill. These quills are now in extremely short supply so substitute quills, as recommended by materials suppliers, will be used. We will need a pair of quills, actually, and that means one quill from the bird's left wing and the other from the right wing. When wing quills are purchased they are bought by the pair, whether they be from the turkey, goose, duck or any other bird. The reason for this is to allow us to tie in a quill segment on one side of the fly which will correspond in texture and conformation to its mate on the other side of the fly. The most critical example of this need is in the case of quill wings which we'll learn in a later chapter. They must be balanced and show a similar relationship to the center line of the fly, which is the hook shank. If one flares outward from the shank, so must the other. If one quill tip points forward, so must the other. To accomplish this on our artificial, we must use a matched pair of feathers.

Here's the procedure for tying the keel tail:

1. Remove a 1/8 to 3/16 inch wide section of quill from the curved side of each feather. Because we want these sections to match each other, we cut them from the same respective position on each quill. Use your scissors to cut these sections free, PHOTO 66.

2. Place the sections next to each other with their *concave* sides together.

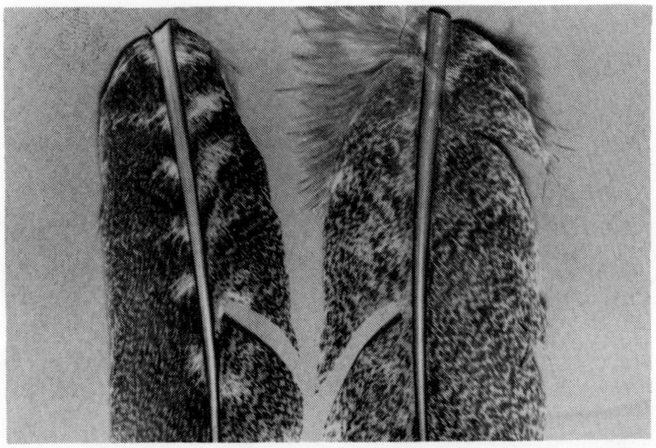

66

3. With your left hand, hold the sections above the shank and tie down exactly as we did for the hackle fiber tail, though not necessarily two gaps long, PHOTO 67. The length and the up-or-down pointing of the tip of this tail is up to you. On Muddlers I don't feel that either of these specifications is of critical importance.

67

I would be remiss here if I didn't mention that many tiers don't take the time to mate two quill sections for this tail. They use a section from only one feather and I'm sure the single section works very nicely. It isn't however, as properly balanced as when tied with the two-section keel technique.

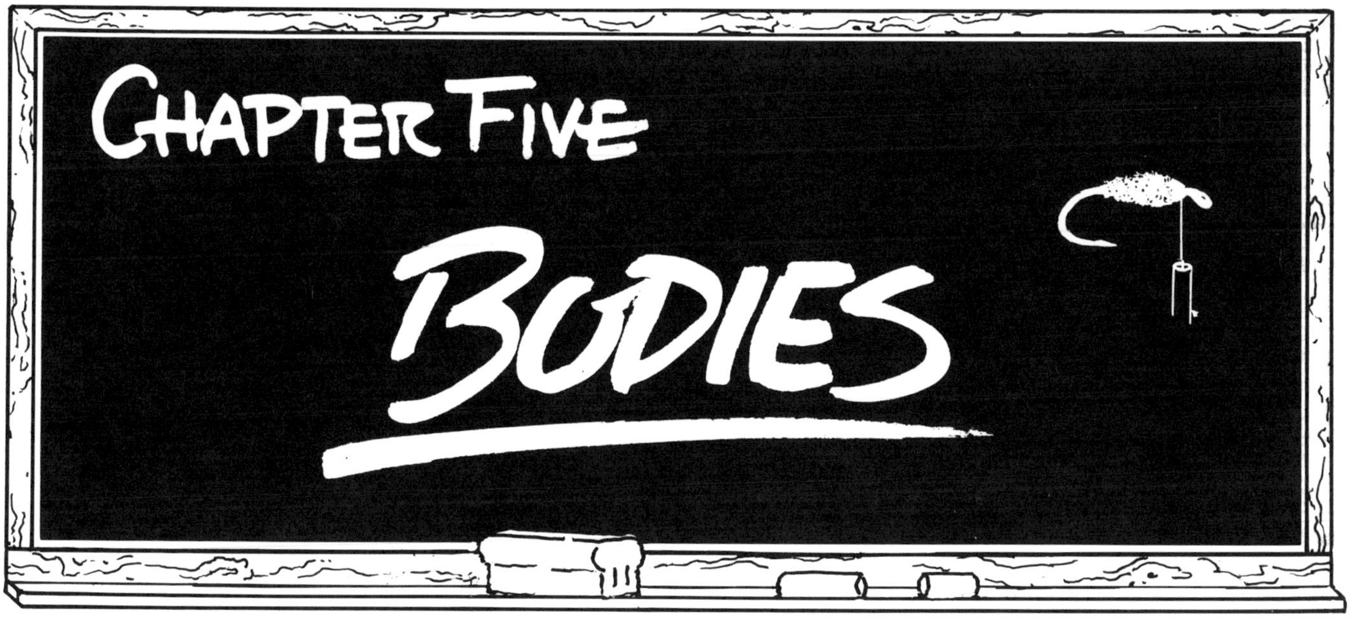

The greatest variety of materials we use in dressing our flies is in the construction of bodies. Tails, wings and hackles, by comparison, utilize relatively few different materials.

General characteristics of fly bodies are few, as are the exceptions to these characteristics. I am listing here those ground rules which are almost always followed, no matter what type of fly is being tied (wet, dry, nymph, etc.).

1. Body length is not determined by a specific formula or by the size of the hook gap, but is necessarily predicated on the length of hook used. We've already determined that hooks are manufactured in a variety of shank lengths within any given size. Spiders are tied on very short shank hooks and damsel fly nymphs are tied on long shank hooks. The *size* of hook may be the same for both of these flies, but the *style* of hook will be much different because the insect configurations are much different.

2. All fly bodies should be applied *tightly* to the hook shank. Most bodies are made from a material which is wound around the shank. Most of these materials, if wound in a loose, casual manner won't survive the chewing of the first fish caught on the fly. Adequate pressure must be applied during the winding procedure to assure the material won't roll laterally around the shank, or slip lengthwise along the shank. Some materials, such as those which are bulky or have a stretchiness to them, can be cemented to the shank to prevent their movement.

Several factors are required to produce fine artificial flies, and one of them is durability! We must always keep this in mind as we construct our flies.

3. Most insect body imitations are tapered in shape; small in diameter at the tail and progressively increasing in diameter toward the head. This increase is subtle but evident. The taper is obvious when examining actual insects both in their larval and adult stages. Exceptions are few and adjustments to the rule can be made where applicable.

4. On patterns tied with a tail, the body material should cover a very small portion of the tail. Carelessly tied flies sometimes have

the tail tie-down thread showing between tail and body. This condition may not impair the effectiveness of the fly as a fish fooler, but it is aesthetically unpleasant to the eye and reflects poorly on the craftsmanship of the tier. The tails of living insects are not magically separated from their bodies, therefore no such magic should be in evidence on our artificials!

As we proceed through this chapter, exceptions to, and amplifications of, these ground rules will be discussed. They are listed here briefly and succinctly because additional discourse is not necessary at this time. The rules are straightforward, easy to comprehend, and should always be borne in mind as you learn to tie so that their application becomes natural and matter-of-fact. I doubt that anything stated in this book can be stated unequivocally. Exceptions can always be found in rare or unusual applications, but my purpose throughout is to establish the *basic* tying ground rules which form a foundation of technique to which the exceptions can then be made.

As we proceed into the step-by-step procedures for different body materials, we'll assume the tail has already been secured to the hook.

FUR BODY—DUBBED

Bodies tied of dubbed animal fur are probably the most commonly used on flies tied to imitate insects whether in the nymphal or adult stage of life. Most insect bodies are of dull, subdued shades of color. So is animal fur. A piece of fur purchased from a materials supplier will have skin which has been tanned to eliminate odor, grease and stiffness. The skin will be soft and easy to work with as would be a section of a discarded fur coat.

To the skin is attached the fur, normally accompanied by stiff guard hairs. To prepare the material for use, we'll proceed as follows using a piece of muskrat fur.

1. Tie a tail to a #12 dry fly hook and let the thread hang at the tail tie-down position.

2. With your scissor tips as close to the skin as practicable, cut a section of fur and hair of about 1/4 inch square from the skin. As you perform this operation, hold the section with your free hand, PHOTO 68.

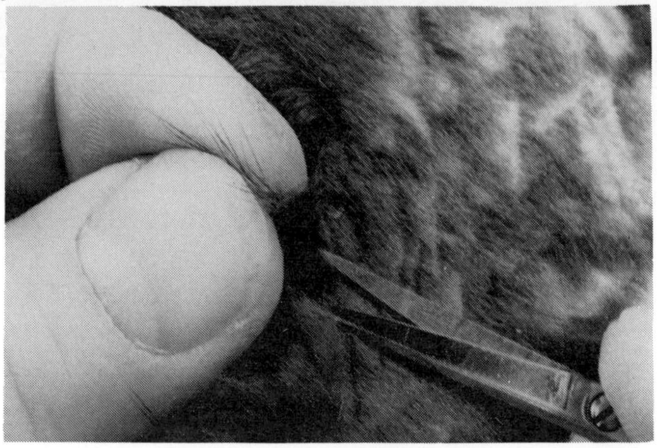

68

3. Now grasp the butt ends (those cut with the scissors) with the thumb and index finger of one hand, and pull out and discard the stiff guard hairs with the other hand. The remaining material is fur only, and is well suited for dry fly bodies as it will apply smoothly and tightly to the hook shank to produce a neat, slender body. (Were you tying a nymph body rather than a dry fly body, you might want to retain the guard hairs in order to produce a fuzzier appearance and texture.)

4. Your next step is to pluck at the fur with your fingertips to take the fibers out of their parallel alignment. We want a very loose fluff-ball of fur with the fibers in disarray, PHOTO 69.

Terminology at this point may be confusing to the novice. The term "dubbing" refers to the material itself (in this case, the muskrat fur). It also refers to the procedure of applying the fur to the thread. We dub fur onto our thread. The fur is dubbing material. To your thread you will now dub on the fur dubbing material. OK? OK!

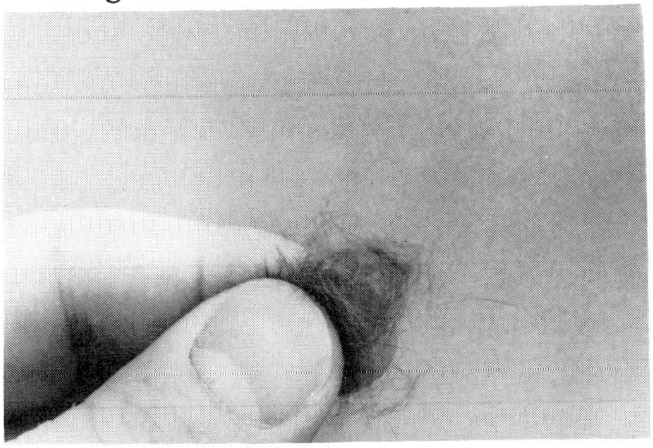

69

Dry fur doesn't adhere well to dry thread. It is desirable, therefore, to be using thread which has been pre-waxed by the manufacturer or waxed by you. If you want to wax your own thread, merely rub a cake of bee's wax or commercial dubbing wax against the four-inch section of thread between the hook and the bobbin. This application will help considerably in making the fur stay in place as it's dubbed.

5. With the bobbin resting in the palm of the left hand, and the fluff of fur held between the thumb and index finger of the left hand, hold tension on the thread. With the thumb and index finger of the right hand grasp a *small* quantity of the fur. I can't stress the *small* too strongly. Press this fur against the thread as close as practicable to the hook. Now pinch and twist the fur and thread in one direction, only, PHOTO 70. This is the act of dubbing! Try to pinch the fur so tightly as to make it part of the thread. Do not roll your fingers back and forth, as the one motion will tighten the fur to the thread while the other motion will tend to loosen it. We wish only to make it tight.

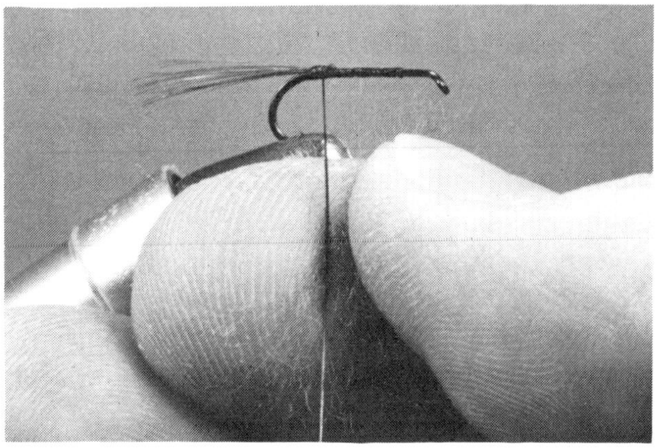

70

6. Now repeat the above procedure with another small clump of fur placed immediately down the thread, but adjacent to the first dubbing. This second clump should blend into the first forming a smooth layer of fur on the thread. Repeat this process until you have dubbed about three to four inches of thread. The fur should now be smooth for its entire length with no voids or no lumpy spots, PHOTO 71.

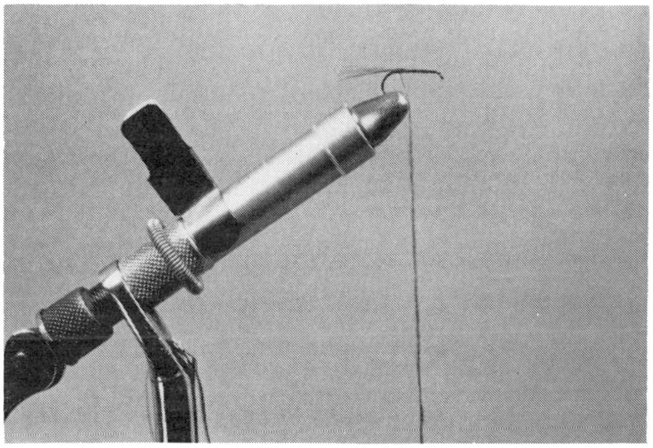

71

7. The bobbin will now be transferred to the right hand and the dubbed thread wound around the shank at the tail so that the fur covers the tail tie-down. The successive winds to the right form the body of the fly, PHOTO 72. Bear in mind that the body must be tapered—small diameter at the tail, growing progressively larger toward the eye of the hook. There are three ways to accomplish this taper:

a. Make the winds of thread progressively closer as you work forward toward the eye to help increase the body diameter.

b. After you've wound completely forward, wind back to the left, and then back forward again if necessary to increase body size. This technique must be performed with care to avoid building up too much fur. Practice here is of unquestioned value.

c. As you dub the fur to the thread, use slightly more fur on each successive application. This will increase the dubbed diameter on the thread, resulting in increased diameter on the shank as it is wound forward.

72

That's the dubbed body! It's really quite simple to accomplish when done in this step-by-step manner. Before you proclaim yourself an expert, however, repeat this technique on several hooks so the procedure won't be forgotten and so you'll form good habits. A razor blade can be used to remove the bodies so the hooks can be used for something else in the future.

For coarser, fuzzier bodies, you may dub the fur in slightly greater quantity and slightly looser—not pinching it quite so tightly to the thread. This approach would be more commonly used when tying wet flies and nymphs as opposed to dry flies.

FUR BODY—THREAD LOCKED

When a very fuzzy fur body is desired for a wet fly, the following technique is often used. Although fur is utilized as the body material, it is not dubbed onto the thread. Instead it is locked between twists of thread in a manner which produces a very shaggy appearance and which can be plucked out with your bodkin point to produce an even fuzzier appearance if desired.

A thread twisting tool is required here and can be easily fashioned from a section of stiff wire. PHOTO 73 shows the tool alongside a ruler. The handle should be three to four inches long. The triple loop tip, forming the thread-holding portion of the tool, measures 7/8 inches across, the large loop being 1/2 inch and the two outer loops being 1/8 inch each.

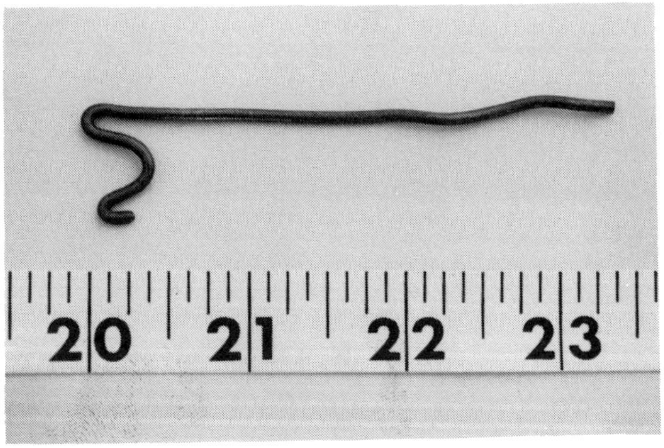

73

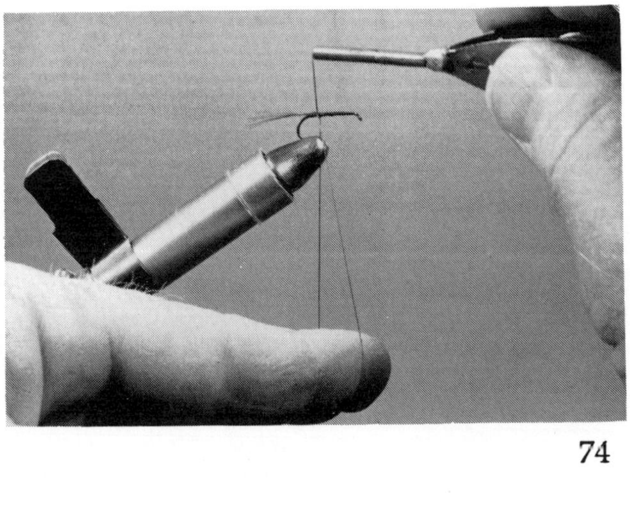

74

We'll proceed as follows:

1. After the tail is in place, pull the bobbin until approximately seven inches of thread is taut between the shank and bobbin tip. With the bobbin in your right hand, place your left index finger on the mid-point of the thread. Bring the bobbin tip up over the hook shank and wind the thread over both ends of the loop securing both to the shank, PHOTO 74. Bring the thread forward to the point where the body will end, and let it hang.

2. Cut some fur from the skin and have it handy on the table. Plucking the guard hairs from the fur is optional, depending on the effect you desire. In the photos I have retained the guard hairs with the fur.

3. Engage the tool into the bottom of the thread loop as shown in PHOTO 75 and twist the tool to the right three or four turns.

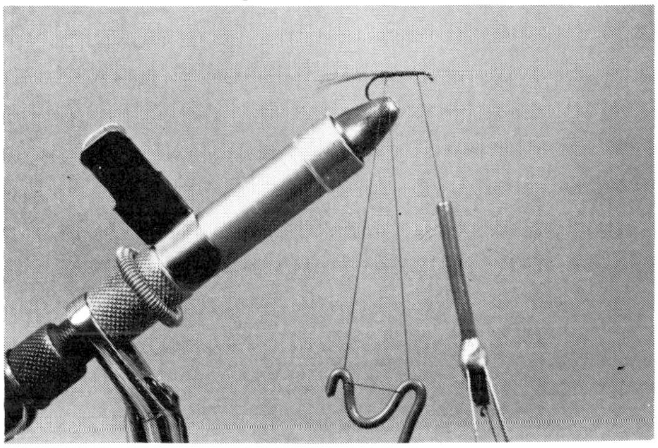

75

4. Holding the twisting tool and the fur in the left hand, place a small portion of fur (with hair) between the loop threads and push up into the twists, PHOTO 76. With your right hand, twist the tool two more turns.

5. Repeat step four until the entire length of the loop has fur caught between the twists. Remember, each time you put the fur between the loop threads, *push* the fur up into the twists.

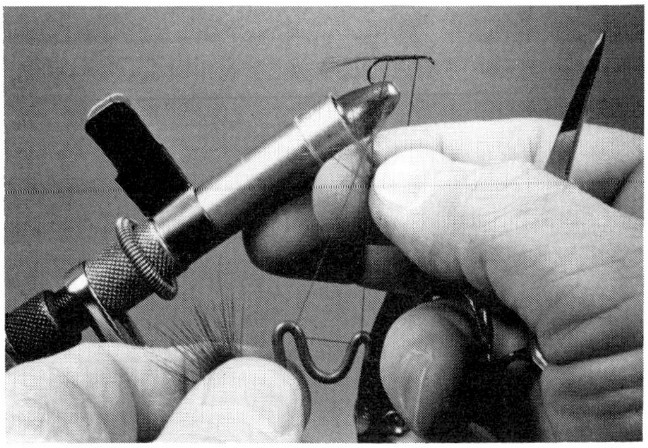

76

6. You'll now wind the body. Holding the bottom of the thread loop with your left hand, remove the tool from the loop and grasp the thread loop with your hackle pliers. This process will close the loop and facilitate the winding. With the pliers in your right hand, wind the thread around the shank and transfer pliers to your left hand under the hook. Now bring the right hand back to the near side of the vise, grasp the pliers with the right hand and wind around the shank again. Repeat this procedure until the body is complete, PHOTO 77. If the body is too fuzzy, trim to shape with your scissors, PHOTO 78. If the body isn't fuzzy enough, pluck out fur and hair with your bodkin point, PHOTO 79.

77

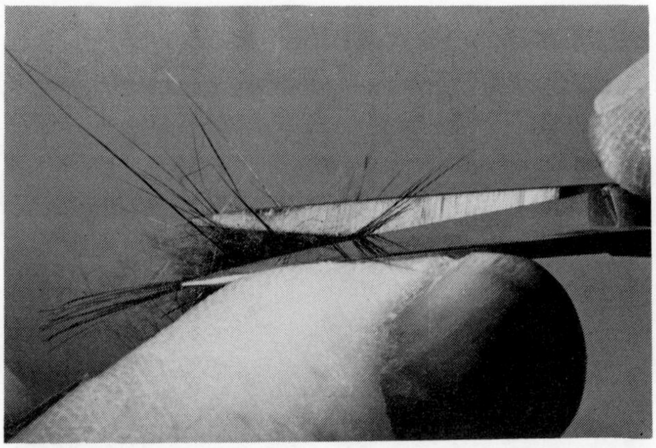

78

79

THE HAIR/FUR BODY

There are two popular fur bodies which fish more effectively when the fur is used in conjunction with its guard hairs. The hair of these two animals is quite short and stiff and not well suited to application by the thread locking method. The two furs under consideration are those from the otter and the English hare's mask. For our practice here we'll use the hare's mask, so popular on the Gold Ribbed Hare's Ear patterns.

When a hare's mask is purchased, you receive the skin from the face of an English hare. Because this mask also includes the ears, we use the hair and fur from them as well as from the face.

1. I prefer to cut the desired fur and hair from the entire mask and store it in a plastic box where it's ready for use when I need it. Cut the black fur and cream hairs from the ears right down to the skin. On the face portion, cut the fur and hair only down to the separating line between the black fur and the tan fur, PHOTO 80. By not cutting down to the skin on the face area, you don't include the tan fur in your dubbing, and the result is a preferred darker body on the artificial fly.

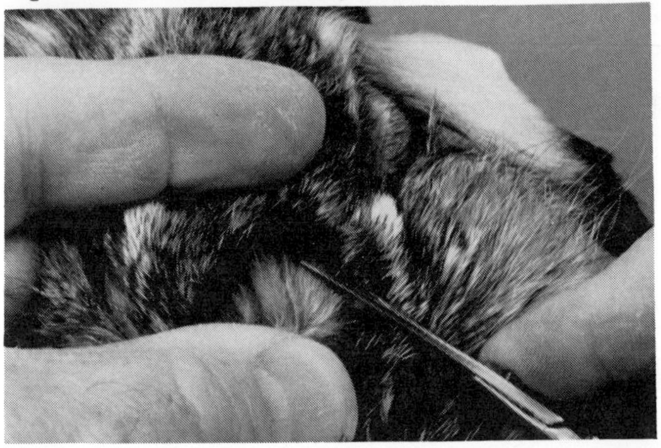

80

2. As you cut off all useable hair and black fur, let it drop onto a newspaper. Now with your fingertips, mix the fur and hair to an even consistency so you don't have clumps of either fur or hair, but rather a uniform blend of both. The color will be a dark brown and the blend will be ready to dub onto your tying thread.

3. Prior to dubbing, apply a *thin* coat of Thompson's Fly Wax to about four inches of your thread with your *middle* finger. This wax is very sticky and is used instead of bee's wax because it will allow the hairs to adhere to the thread much better than would the less tacky bee's wax.

4. Now dub the hair/fur mixture to the thread just as you did the muskrat fur, except

your result on the thread will be decidedly coarser than the muskrat. You want the hairs to protrude randomly from the fly body, PHOTO 81.

81

5. Wind the dubbing around the shank to form a tapered body. For the Gold Ribbed Hare's Ear fly, the body will be ribbed with gold wire or narrow gold tinsel. (See major heading "Ribbing" in this chapter.)

THE QUILL BODY

Fly bodies dressed with a quill material offer a hard, segmented appearance and a slender profile. These characteristics closely resemble the bodies of many adult insects and therefore this type of artificial body is in evidence on many artificial flies.

A quill is really nothing more than a solid strand of semi-rigid material which we wind around the shank of the hook with each wind lying immediately adjacent to or slightly overlapping the previous wind. Quills we use usually are from the feather of a bird or the hair from an animal. We do, however, also use synthetic material such as nylon monofilament for the same purpose.

Popular fly patterns such as the Gordon Quill, Ginger Quill, and Blue Quill all utilize a quill from the tail feather of a peacock, and we'll use this quill to practice the tying technique (see Materials Directory for other options).

From a tackle shop or tying materials catalog you would order an "eyed peacock tail feather" to obtain this material. You would receive a feather from one to three feet long (possibly cut into sections for convenience) composed of a white main stem (quill) from which would protrude many other delicate quills up to six inches long. These latter quills are what we use. They are covered with green/bronze fuzz called herl. The herl itself is used on many effective fly patterns, but at the moment we are concerned only with the quill portion and will therefore remove the herl.

Cut or pull one of the fragile, herl-covered quills from the main white stem. Those quills, starting just below the eye of the feather down about 2/3 the length of the stem length, are the easiest to work with. The quills near the butt of the stem are usually very fragile. Those in the eye itself have the most definitive longitudinal markings, resulting in the best segmented appearance when used for the fly body, but they are very short and the herl is difficult to remove (see Chapter Eight for this removal technique.)

The end of the quill which had been attached to the stem is referred to as the "butt" end. If you have an average thumbnail, lay the quill across the side of the tip section of your right index finger. Press your thumb nail down on the quill and pull the quill with your left hand so that your thumbnail scrapes down toward the butt, PHOTO 82. You should notice that some of the herl has been scraped from the quill. Repeat this process until the butt end has about four inches of bare quill showing. Because the tip of the quill is so fragile, we use the stronger butt end for winding the body. Should you have no thumbnail, or find its use ineffective in performing this step, you may lay the quill on a hard surface and stroke the herl from tip to butt with an eraser. This technique is effective, but it's usually more time consuming than using the thumbnail.

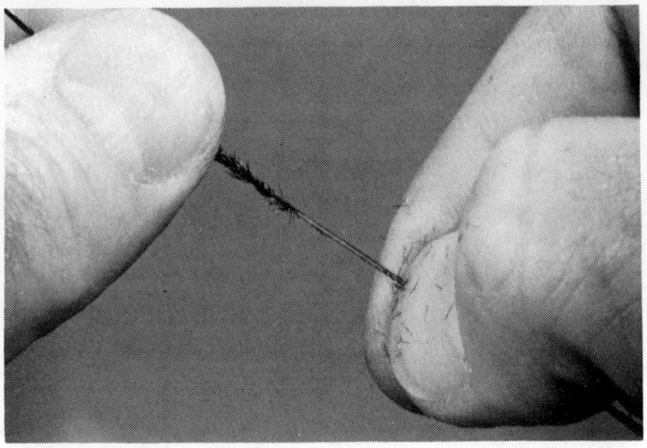

82

You'll notice the stripped quill is tapered from tip to butt and is flat in cross-section. These two points are important relative to the quill's use as a fly body.

You should also notice that the quill has two shades of color running lengthwise on each of its flat sides. This color difference is more distinct on the "eye" quills than it is on the quills farther down the stem. At any rate, this difference is what gives the completed body a segmented appearance. Natural insect bodies are segmented and the segments are narrower at the tail, becoming progressively wider toward the head. To represent this progressive widening, you will tie the narrowest portion of the quill to the hook prior to winding the quill around the shank to form the body.

If you wound this flat quill around a constant diameter hook shank, your result would be a constant diameter fly body. We don't want that—we want a tapered body. Therefore, we must first wind our *thread* to form the taper. The total procedure for tying the peacock quill body is as follows:

1. After the tail has been completed, lay the small end of the bare quill against the near side of the shank, at the tail, with the quill pointing up and to the left.

2. Wind thread over the quill tip to secure it to the shank. If the quill wants to roll around the hook shank when you start these winds of thread, grasp the quill very close to the tie-down location and release tension on the thread for the first turn only. This trick usually allows you to get that first wind cinched down over the quill before it can roll.

3. Now wind the thread up and down the shank to form a slight taper and let the thread hang at the front of the body, PHOTO 83.

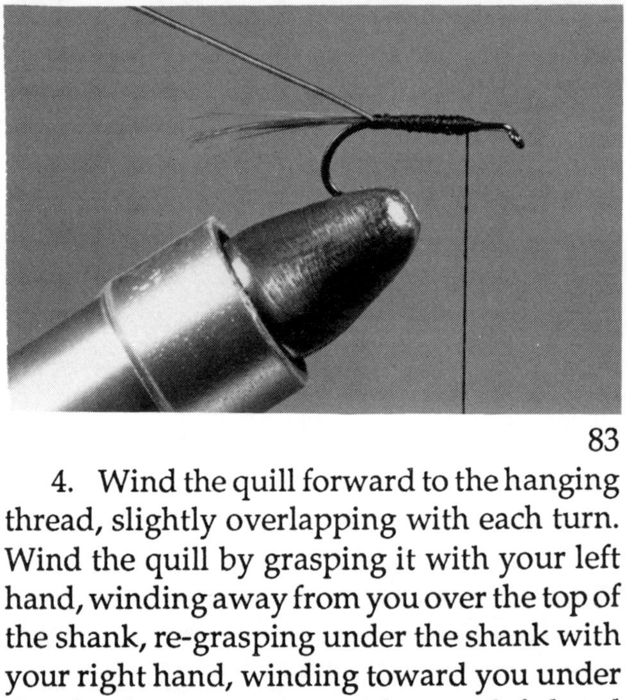

83

4. Wind the quill forward to the hanging thread, slightly overlapping with each turn. Wind the quill by grasping it with your left hand, winding away from you over the top of the shank, re-grasping under the shank with your right hand, winding toward you under the shank, re-grasping with your left hand and repeat all of the above. Where the body is to stop, hold the quill with the *right* hand, wind two turns of thread around the quill and shank with the left hand, PHOTO 84, and finish securing the quill to the shank with three or four more winds of thread with the right hand. Trim the stub of quill close to the shank. The body is complete—tight, tapered and segmented.

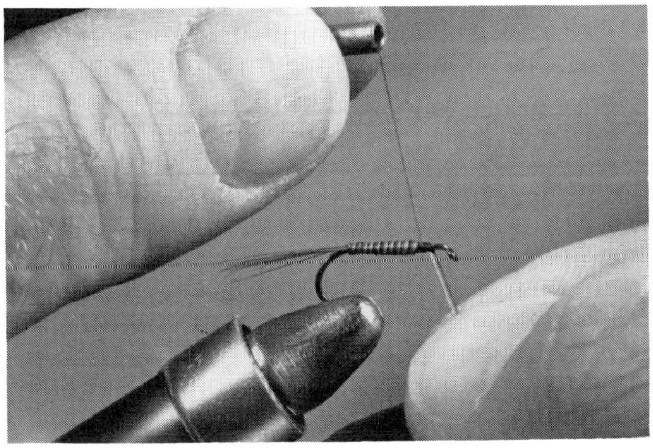

84

Because this body is very fragile and susceptible to breaking at the slightest touch from a fish's tooth, quill bodies should be coated with an application of head cement when the *fly* is *complete.* We don't coat the body when only the body is complete, because we'd have to wait for the cement to dry before we could proceed with the next step, which is usually the winding of the hackle. The most efficient way to apply the cement is with the bodkin point. Merely rub the cement-coated point along the length of the body until it's completely covered.

The Materials Directory section of this book lists a hackle quill as another material which can be used for quill bodies so I'll explain here the preparation of this material. Remove a large feather from a hackle neck of your choice. Remove the hackle fibers from the quill by pulling them down toward the quill butt. You now have a tapered quill which will be tied to the shank by the tip end and wound forward with tight turns. Because the diameter of the quill is progressively larger as you wind forward, you have an automatic body taper without the necessity of the thread-taper process used with the flat peacock quill. Tie off the quill in the same manner as you did the peacock, and the body is complete, PHOTO 85.

When using any quill material, you will occasionally find the material is dry, brittle, and prone to breaking as it's wound tightly around the shank. To alleviate this problem, soak the quills in warm water for a few minutes prior to use.

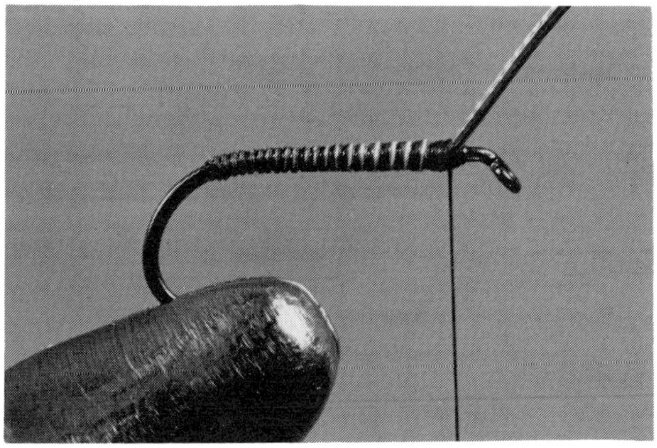

85

86

THE TINSEL BODY

Tinsel is a narrow (1/16 to 1/8 inch) metal or mylar strip which is sold on spools or wrapped on cards. It is normally silver or gold in color and is used either as a primary body material or as a ribbing material (technique for tying is coming up soon).

It is tied in, wound around the shank, and tied off just as we did with the peacock quill. The exception to this likeness is a tapered cut we make to the end we tie in, PHOTO 86. This taper is made for a couple of reasons: first, to reduce any unwanted bulk at the point of tie-down and second, to reduce the possibility of cutting the thread on the sharp edge of the tinsel because it lays out over the edge of the shank. This latter consideration is most valid when we are using wide metal tinsel.

An underbody to form a taper normally is not required because the tinsel body is more of an attractor type rather than an imitator of a specific insect body.

RIBBING

A rib on the body of a fly is a second material wound spirally over the main body material giving the body a segmented appearance. A secondary value of the rib is that it helps strengthen the body and hold it together.

The rib material most commonly used has been a gold or silver tinsel, but several other items may be used as noted in the Materials Directory. No matter what you choose to use, it should be remembered that the rib *accents* the main body material, it doesn't dominate it. In other words you should see more body material than rib material when viewing the completed fly.

To be traditional, we'll use tinsel for our illustration and wind it over a dubbed fur body.

1. After the tail has been completed, cut a four-inch section of tinsel from the spool at a taper and lay the taper against your side of the hook and tie down exactly as you did for the peacock quill body.

2. The tinsel will not be used while dubbing the body, so place it back into your material clip until needed, PHOTO 87. The dubbed fur body is now wound and the thread will be hanging at the front end of the body.

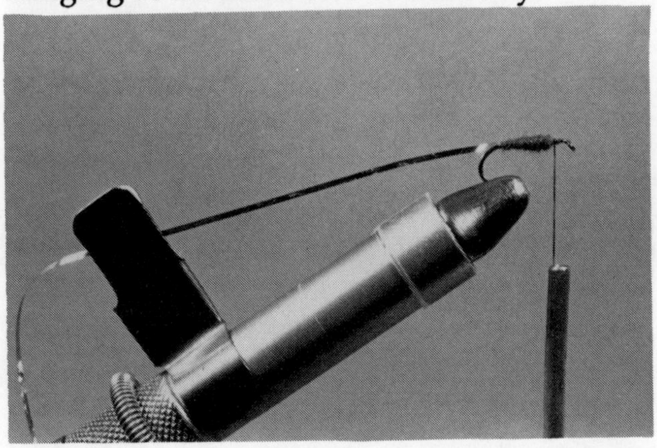

87

3. Remove the tinsel from the clip and wind it tightly forward over the body, making sure the body material dominates the tinsel. When the tinsel reaches the forward end of the body, hold it in your right hand and tie off as you did with the quills. PHOTO 88 shows a ribbed body. Caution is again advised to take care not to cut your thread on the tinsel edges.

88

Let me note here that ribs should *always* be wound over peacock quill and peacock herl bodies. As mentioned previously, these materials are very fragile, and the rib helps to prevent their unraveling. A *reverse* rib is called for over quill bodies, which means the rib material is wound in a counter-clockwise direction rather than the customary clockwise direction we use for the vast majority of our tying procedures. Merely wind the rib toward you over the top of the shank rather than away from you, which is customary.

The normal procedure for winding material forward from tail toward head places the material at a slightly forward-leaning angle on the shank. The reverse rib creates a cross-hatch effect for greater durability.

FLAT MONOFILAMENT BODY

Unlike the tinsel, with its silver or gold reflective surface, flat monofilament is a translucent material used either in its natural clear hue or dyed to any desired color. It is used as a ribbing material or as the exterior body material when a translucent segmented appearance is desired. In either case it is normally wound over another material such as floss or yarn. When used as the primary exterior of a body, a clear mono will allow the underbody color to be most visible.

Flat mono is available in size 18 pound test and larger and, because of its size, is normally used on hooks of size #10 and larger, assuming the shank is of regular length or longer.

The technique for using this material is to tie it in at the tail prior to forming the body or underbody, then winding as desired over the body material, and tying off as we did the quill and tinsel. Because its smooth surface offers the potential for pulling out from the tie-down, I'd recommend the application of a drop of head cement on the shank at each point of tie-down to create added durability.

THE PEACOCK HERL BODY

The herl you removed from the peacock quill to tie the quill body is left intact when tying flies which call for a peacock herl body. Flies such as the Royal Coachman, Brown Hackle Peacock, and Renegade require the use of this herl, and to tie such a body is quite easy, and is done as follows:

1. Remove two or three quills from the stem. The number of quills can vary from one to eight depending on the length of shank we must cover but two or three is good for most size #12 and #14 hooks.

2. Tie in all quills at the same time in the manner you did the quill body, tying down their tip ends at the tail of the fly. The tips are weak, so tie in at least an inch back from the very end of the quills, PHOTO 89.

89

3. Wind the thread forward to the point at which you want the body to end and let it hang.

4. Wind all quills forward at the same time and tie off together in the same manner as you did the quill body. This body will normally make its own taper as you wind forward because the herl fibers become progressively longer from the tip of the quill to the butt.

THE FLOSS BODY

To my mind, floss is one of the most

frustrating of body materials to use. It's normally made of silk or rayon and each floss strand is made up of hundreds of tiny filaments. When winding, these filaments tend to break and separate, particularly if the tier's fingers are rough.

Several patterns of flies call for floss bodies and its use should be mastered. When spooled at the factory, floss is wound in one, two, and four-strand increments. I prefer to purchase the four-strand type because each strand is very small in diameter. Fly bodies can then be tied using from one to four strands at a time, depending on the size of the hook. Single-strand floss is usually much too bulky for use on small hooks.

As opposed to the manner in which we tied the fur, quill, and herl bodies, I prefer to wind the floss from front to rear, then back forward again. The total procedure is as follows:

1. With a thread base wound on the hook shank, tie in a four-inch strand of floss (use one strand only on a #12 hook) at the *front* end of the body, PHOTO 90. Before tying, the tip of the floss should be moistened between your lips to prevent the fibers from fraying. The reason for tying in at this position is to avoid excessive bulk near the tail. Since the body is to be trimly tapered, tying in at this position is logical.

90

2. Wind the floss back to the start of the bend, then wind forward to where the thread is hanging, tapering the body as you wind. Tie off, PHOTO 91.

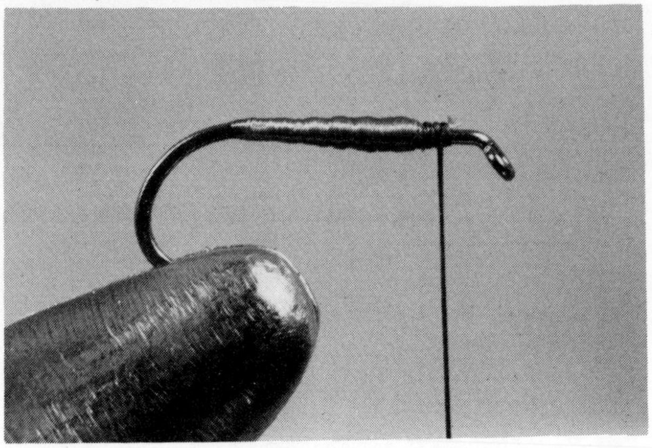

91

3. For durability, this body is usually ribbed. Another good practice is to place a small drop of head cement at the junction of the body and tail to prevent the filaments of the floss from slipping down over the tail making the fly ineffective. The body itself, however, would not be cemented or lacquered over.

You will read about, and see listed in catalogs, a type of floss called acetate floss. It, too, comes in many colors and looks and feels like silk and rayon floss. The difference is in its ability to "melt" when placed into a solution of acetone. The floss doesn't dissolve, but rather becomes pliable and capable of being moulded to a desired shape such as into a flat body. After a few minutes, the "melted" floss will dry to a hard body of the shape formed. A standard method of forming is to squeeze the floss with a pair of tweezers or small pliers.

There is one particular problem which arises occasionally when winding any floss, and because I'm sure it occurs even at the vise of the most expert fly tiers, I want to explain its solution.

The problem is a flaring and separation of the floss filaments, PHOTO 92, from their otherwise closely compacted configuration.

The reason for this separation is because at some stage of winding the body, the floss strand winds around an uneven circumference on the hook shank. At this point, our nice thread-like strand of floss starts to flare. Fear not, the remedy is very simple.

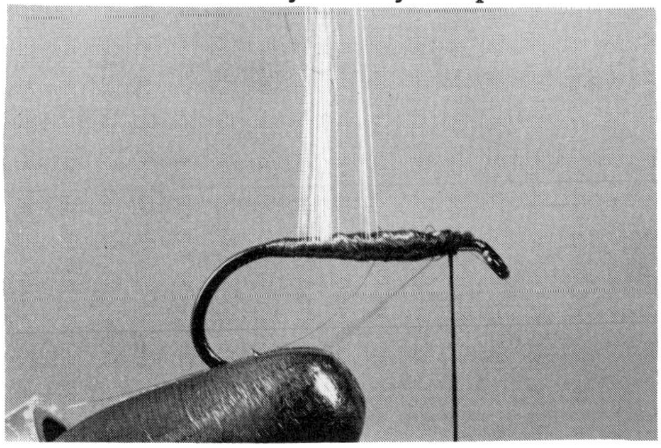

92

With your left thumbnail press slightly into the floss as in PHOTO 93. This action will compact the filaments. Now make one wind around the body while pressing. Repeat if necessary. The problem has been easily cured!

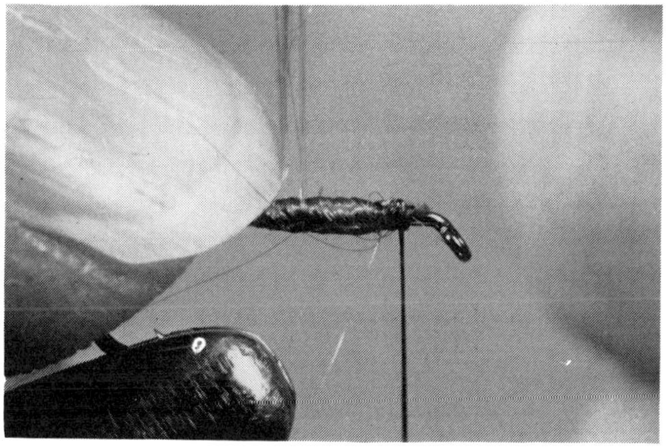

93

THE YARN BODY

Wool, Mohlon, mohair, spun fur, etc. are all yarn-like in nature. They are single or multiple strand materials, relatively coarse or fuzzy in appearance, and considerably larger in diameter than floss. I don't recommend them for the tying of dry fly bodies as they are quite water absorbant. They do, however, have value in tying nymphs and other wet fly patterns.

The construction of these bodies is very simple. The material is tied in either at the tail or the front end of the body, depending on the diameter desired, wound around the shank as you did the floss, and tied off.

These yarns are usually of such bulky proportions that they will overpower a standard length hook of size #14 and smaller. The bodies would be too large in relationship to the rest of the fly. If you would insist on using one of these materials for small flies, you may, but I suggest you do so in the following manner. Rather than winding the yarn in its natural state as previously described, the yarn can either be plucked with the fingernails, or cut into short (1/2 to 3/4 inch) sections and spun in a kitchen blender. Either of these techniques will result in a fluff of fibers resembling fur dubbing. This material will be dubbed onto the thread, as we do fur, and wound around the shank to form the body. Another advantage of these two procedures is that different colors can be mixed and blended into desired colors not available in the material's original yarn form.

CHENILLE BODY

This popular wet fly body material is sold in several diameters, is wound around the shank just as the yarns would be, but usually no taper is attempted. The fibers of chenille are extremely short and blending of colors is not possible as with the yarn-type materials. There are, however, variegated chenilles available, or two strands of different colored chenille can be tied in together and wound around the shank together, giving the body a striped appearance, PHOTO 94.

94

POLYPROPYLENE BODY

This manufactured fiber has become a boon to the tier of dry flies as it has a specific gravity of less than 1.0, making it a material which floats very well. It is produced in many "buggy" colors, allowing the tier to easily represent many insect body colors, and it is available commercially either as a yarn or as a fluff of dubbing material. The latter form very nicely facilitates our mixing of colors in a blender to achieve "custom" colors for more precise representations.

CLIPPED HAIR BODY

The hair of many animals is used in the dressing of artificial flies and it can be used in one way or another to represent any part of a fly's anatomy. In the case of the clipped body, the hair used is normally deer, elk or caribou. The former is the most popular and we'll use it in learning this type of body construction. These three hairs are hollow and therefore offer us the opportunity to use a natural fiber which possesses excellent floating characteristics. A pattern such as the Irresistible, which utilizes deer hair in the tail, body, and wings, is a very popular fly in the West because it floats well in the rough water of fast moving streams. Deer hair is "spun" around the shank of the hook, packed tight, then clipped with scissors to the shape desired. The procedure is as follows:

1. Insert a #8 dry fly hook into the vise. Attach a strong 3/0 thread just forward of the bend of the hook, PHOTO 95. I prefer a grey or tan thread to closely match the color of the hair. Nylon is used because of its strength, which is normally required whenever we work with hair. We want to leave as much of the shank as possible free of thread at this point to facilitate our "spinning" of the hair, as it will spin easily on the bare metal, but not on a thread base.

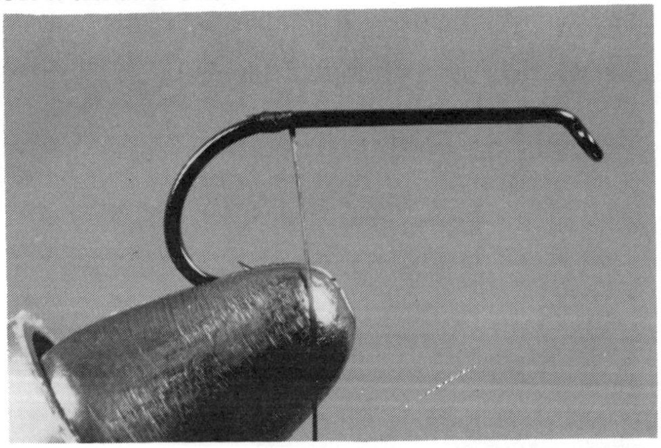

95

2. From the deer hide, cut about 30 hairs using your scissor tips. You will normally find a small quantity of under fur at the base of these hairs. Pull out this fur using a fine toothed comb.

3. With your scissors, cut the *points* from the fibers, leaving a hair bundle about 3/4 inch long.

4. With your left hand, hold the bundle

parallel to, and about 1/8 inch above, the shank of the hook with the middle of the bundle directly over your hanging thread, PHOTO 96.

96

5. Attach the fibers to the hook shank in the same manner in which you attached the tail fibers in Chapter Four. Now continue to wind the thread tightly around the shank. As you do so, the hair will both spin and flare, distributing itself rather evenly around the shank. This flaring effect will stop after two or three turns of thread, PHOTO 97. When it does, you stop winding because you want the build-up of thread on the shank to be as minimal as possible. Now with your left hand, gently pull *all* of the hairs to your left and wind two turns of thread around the bare shank immediately in front (to the right) of the hair. This procedure will prevent the turns around the hair from loosening.

97

6. With the nails of your right thumb and middle finger, push this section of fibers to your left in an effort to compact them as tightly as possible, PHOTO 98.

98

7. Now repeat steps two through six again. This second bundle will be tied down immediately adjacent to the first bundle.

8. Continue this tying-and-compacting procedure until the thread hangs approximately 1/4 shank length back from the eye of the hook. Now place two half-hitch knots in front of the deer hair, PHOTO 99.

99

9. At this point in the process, you can practice your skill at giving a haircut. The body must now be clipped with your scissors to the shape desired. As with other body types, you want to trim the hair to form a tapered body. To save time, don't be timid! Bring the points of your scissors into the hairs from your right

to your left, close to the shank, and at a slight angle to form the taper, PHOTO 100. Now cut!

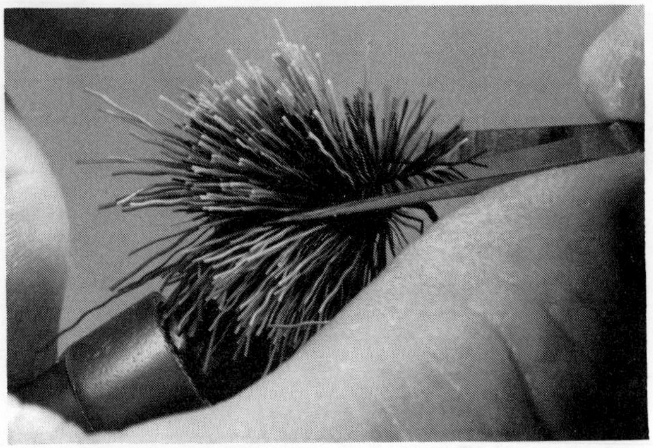

100

10. Rotate the sleeve of your vise and repeat step nine. You will cut entirely around the body until you have a rough approximation of the shape and size of the final form of the body, PHOTO 101. Now the final touch-up clipping will be done to assure all blunt ends of hair are cut down to the length you desire. Use proper caution in these final stages of shaping to assure you don't cut your thread. It's a frustrating experience, and can occur rather easily as you rotate the vise sleeve because the thread tends to wind around the body into perfect position to be inadvertently severed.

101

The above ten steps taught you to tie the clipped hair body without the tail in position. At this point I need to make some comments about tying this body after the tail has been set in place.

The main problem encountered in spinning hair with the tail in position is that your first bundle or two of fibers will *not* be tied down on the bare metal shank. They must be tied down on the thread which secures the tail, and this thread prevents the smooth and even spinning action of the hair which we experienced on the bare shank.

To overcome this problem, it is necessary for us to manually distribute the hair around the shank. This is not a difficult maneuver and is accomplished in the following way.

1. With the tail secure and the thread hanging below its base, set the bundle of body hair down on the shank with the middle of the bundle above the hanging thread, PHOTO 102.

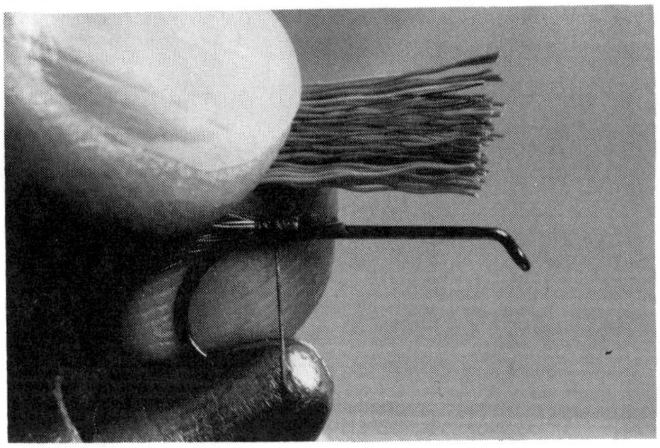

102

2. With the thumb and index finger of the left hand, wiggle and move and manipulate the fibers so as to force them to be equally distributed around the circumference of the hook, PHOTO 103.

3. Now wind the tying thread around the hairs with three tight turns of thread to secure them to the shank. Those hairs extending to the right of the tie-down will now be pushed to the left to make them flare out perpendicular to the shank. Bring the thread forward,

wind twice around the shank and allow it to hang immediately adjacent to, and in front of, these flared hairs.

103

4. If the tail tie-down thread is still showing, repeat steps one through three. Normally no more than two bundles will be required to cover the tail thread with hair. From this point forward, the previously described spinning technique will be used to complete the body.

Two additional factors should be stressed at this juncture. The first conveys the reason for trimming off the hair points before securing the hair bundle to the hook shank. When the body shaping is being done with your scissors, it is far easier to differentiate the tail hairs, if they are deer also, from the body hairs, if all the body hairs have blunt ends. It gets a bit tedious to trim the body when both body and tail hairs look identical!

The second comment worth consideration concerns durability of this body. To assure that the clipped hair won't loosen and rotate around the shank after being fished for some time, I like to apply a small drop of head cement to the shank at the point of, and just prior to, securing each hair bundle to the shank. The hair will spin without difficulty in the liquid cement, but will remain very stationary after the cement dries.

THE MYLAR PIPING BODY

Some fly patterns, most frequently those used for warm water or salt water fishing, call for a body of silver or gold braided mylar piping (also called tubing). This material reminds us of a form of heavy cord such as sometimes is used to wrap gifts. It is made of very narrow mylar tinsel, braided into a hollow tube configuration around a core of string-like material which allows the tube to retain its shape, but still remain flexible.

This body has the flash and reflective characteristics of standard tinsel bodies and at the same time presents a better representation of the scale pattern which would be natural on a small fish.

The tying procedure is as follows:

1. Attach the thread at the rear of a long shank hook (let's use a #8, #79580) immediately in front of the bend. Build an untapered underbody of floss or yarn. This underbody will not be visible when the fly is complete, but merely acts as a base over which you will slip the tube of mylar. Return the thread to the rear of the underbody, PHOTO 104.

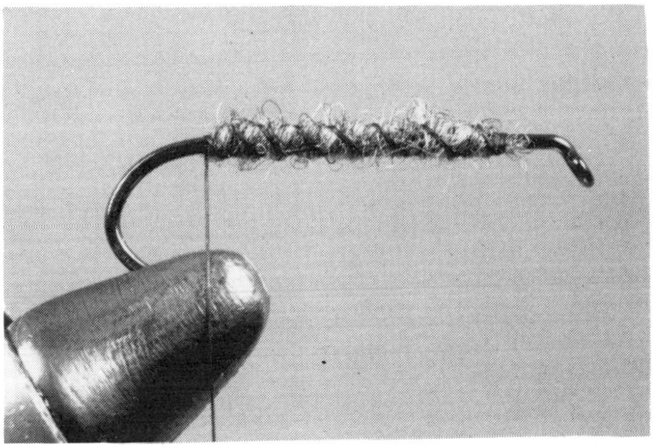

104

2. Cut a section of the tubing one inch longer than the length you wish to make the completed body. Remove the string core.

3. Slip the tubing over the eye of the hook

and underbody. Wind the thread over the tube end on the braided portion to bind the tubing securely to the shank, PHOTO 105. Tie a whip finish knot with your fingers, not the tool, and cut the thread free from the fly.

105

4. Attach the thread to the shank at the front of the underbody and wind over the tube end to again secure the tubing to the shank. Tie a half hitch knot, PHOTO 106.

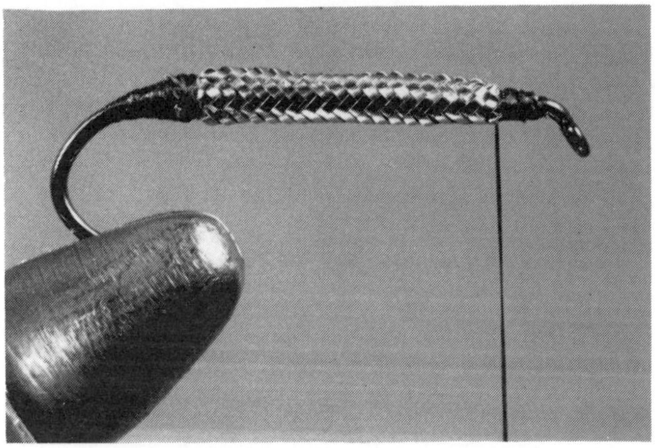

106

5. At this stage the body is complete and the thread is in position to proceed to the next step of the fly which might be a wing or a hackle.

6. When the fly has been completed, you should apply two coats of head cement to the rear and front mylar tie-downs to assure the windings won't fray or pull loose while fishing.

A MULTI-SECTION BODY

Some fly bodies are more involved than merely tying one material from tail to head. Such bodies may involve two or more colors of the same material or two or more different materials. A perfect example of such a body is that of the Royal Coachman, one of the best known fly patterns in the world. This body is composed of two materials—peacock herl and red floss—applied in such a manner as to form a three-section body. The floss forms the center section, while the peacock forms a front and rear egg sac. Each of the sections could be tied in, wound, and tied off as separate entities; but a bit of foresight has produced the following method, which I feel is quicker, yet just as durable as the three-entity process.

1. Place a #12 dry fly hook in your vise. Cover the shank with thread and let the thread hang at the tail position.

2. In your left hand, hold two strands of red floss plus one peacock quill with herl intact. Lay all three against your side of the hook shank at the tail, and tie in, PHOTO 107.

107

3. Wind the thread forward 1/8 inch. Pull the floss strands forward and wind three turns of thread over them to hold them in place, PHOTO 108.

108

4. Wind the herl around the shank from the tail up to the hanging thread and tie the herl down. Now wind the thread forward again about 1/4 inch, pull herl forward and tie it down with three turns of thread, PHOTO 109.

109

5. Wind the floss forward to form the mid-section of the body and tie it down at the point where the thread is hanging, PHOTO 110.

110

6. Because the floss is no longer needed, cut it off close to the shank. Wind the thread forward 1/8 inch and let it hang. Wind the herl forward to form the front egg sac, tie it down, and cut off the excess herl. The body is now complete, PHOTO 111.

111

By tying the body in this manner, you have saved the time required to tie in the floss and forward herl separately as well as the time required to cut off the excess herl from the rear egg sac.

You'll notice from the photographs that the floss section is greater in length than either of the egg sacs. These proportions are standard, and would vary only if long or short shanked hooks were used. The floss section is proportionately much longer for example, when tying the Royal Coachman Streamer.

The hackle of an artificial fly is normally composed of many fibers from the feather of a bird. Most flies utilize hackle feathers from the head and neck of chickens, sometimes referred to as gamecocks. Many of the birds used for wet flies are wild chickens grown in India, China and the Philippines. The male birds produce feathers best suited for use on dry flies and the hen feathers are suited only to hackles on wet flies. In recent years tiers have had available to them feathers from chickens domestically grown especially for the fly tying trade. They are usually graded as #1, #2 and #3 quality and all are designed for use on dry flies.

Hackle feathers are almost always purchased on the skin, which is referred to as a "hackle neck." When an exceptionally long feather is required, as when winding the feather around the full length of the fly body, the feather may be taken from what is known as a "saddle patch." This is a piece of skin and its attendant feathers from the rump area of a cock chicken. These feathers are not normally used for collar hackles due to the long length of the individual fibers, but they do work well on larger patterns where short fiber length is not critical.

Wet fly hackles are sometimes tied with selected body feathers from birds such as partridge and grouse because these feathers, like those from the hen hackle neck, are soft, supple, and water absorbant.

A dry fly hackle serves two main purposes on the fly. It is the primary material which enables the fly to float, and it can give the impression of insect legs resting on the water's surface film. Because we want our dry flies to float as well as possible, I recommend you purchase the best hackle necks you can obtain. Finding a truly fine dry neck is a real problem in the moderate price ranges, but if you have the opportunity to inspect necks at a retail outlet, look them over carefully and choose the best you can find. As for the high quality domestic necks, a #2 is usually very satisfactory for dry fly tying. Characteristics to look for in a dry fly hackle in order of their importance are as follows:

1. Short, stiff fibers
2. As little webby material as possible
3. Long, slender feathers
4. High gloss, or sheen, to the outside surface of the feathers

5. Small diameter quill

These characteristics are not only important to the floating capability of the fly's hackle, but also reflect on the quality of the hackle fiber tails we tie.

In selecting dry fly necks, the quantity of feathers on the skin (cape) should always be subordinate to their quality. With wet fly necks, this rule need not apply.

Because you must know the names given to different hackle types, PHOTO 112 shows six of the most common hackles tied. Top row, left to right: collar hackle, fore and aft hackle and palmered hackle. Bottom row, left to right: bi-visible, parachute and throat (beard) hackles.

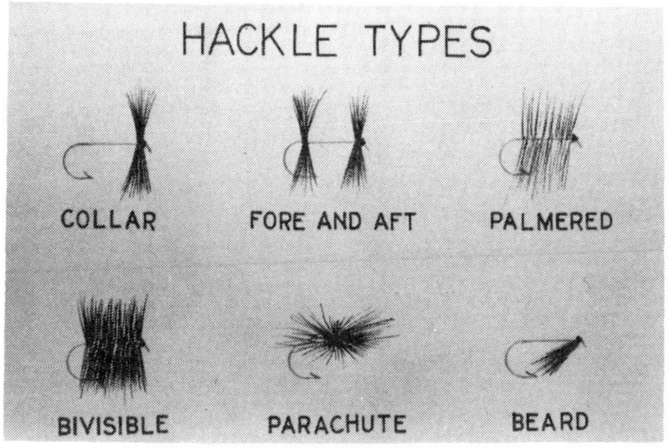

112

The collar, fore and aft, and palmered hackles may be tied on both wet and dry patterns. The bi-visible and parachute styles are strictly for dries. The throat style is strictly wet and technically is not a hackle as such, but rather it is a hackle material tied in beneath the hook shank to represent the legs of an insect.

COLLAR HACKLE—DRY FLY

The collar hackle is by far the most important style in tying the traditional patterns, so let's tie it first. Normally two feathers will be used unless the neck we are using provides us with very long, slender feathers. Before we start the actual preparation and winding of the feathers, I want to list the important general characteristics of a good dry fly collar hackle (further explanation will follow as we move through the chapter):

1. The fibers should measure 1 and 1/2 gaps in length from the quill out to the tip of the fiber.

2. Use two feathers of the same size.

3. The fibers should extend from the hook shank in a plane essentially perpendicular to the shank.

4. The winds of the feathers must be made as close together as possible, forcing the hackle to take very little space along the length of the shank.

Let's proceed now to the preparation of the feathers and the actual winding of the hackle.

1. For the purpose of this practice session, we'll use a #12 hook already dressed with a tail and a dubbed fur body. You'll note from the photographs that the body extends from the tail to within approximately 1/4 shank length from the eye. This bare shank section will accommodate the hackle and head. Your thread should be hanging from the shank at the front of the body.

2. As a beginning fly tier, you should use a hackle gauge to help familiarize yourself with the area on the neck from which to select your two feathers. For starters, remove two feathers which are attached to the skin about two inches up from the "top" (small end) of the hackle neck, PHOTO 113. Dress each feather down entirely. With your hackle gauge lying

on the table in front of you, lay the feather on the gauge so the midpoint of the quill is on the right-hand end of the horizontal line under which you read the number 12, PHOTO 114. This number represents the hook size we are tying. Note the feather quill is *not* parallel with the gauge. This angled position is necessary because we want the *fiber* to be parallel to the horizontal line. This line measures 1 and 1/2 gaps length for a #12 hook. If the fiber, from its tip to the quill is the same length as the line, we have the proper feather. If the fiber is longer than the line, this feather will be suitable for a larger hook size. If shorter, it can be used on a smaller hook. Some trial and error may be necessary to find the proper feathers!

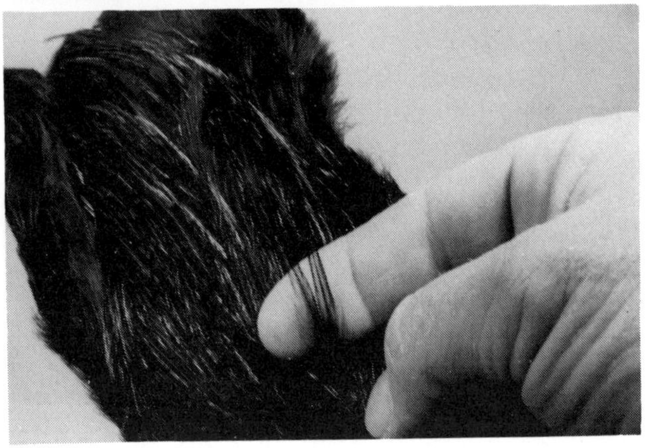

113

114

Some tiers will pluck all the suitable feathers from an entire neck and file them in a compartmented plastic box by size. The compartments may be labeled from size #10 to size #20 or smaller. When tying, the tier has the proper feathers immediately available without the need to pluck and measure. Pre-sizing hackle in this manner is great practice toward learning proper feather size merely by looking at the feather, with no need to use the gauge.

3. With two feathers now properly measured for our #12 hook, strip away all the downy and webby fibers near the butt of the quill until the only fibers remaining are at least 3/4 pure stiff fiber, with no more than 1/4 of the fiber containing web adjacent to the quill, PHOTO 115.

115

4. You're now ready to tie the feathers to the hook shank at the front of the fur body. Hold the two feathers together between the thumb and index finger of the left hand. The position of the feathers will be with the shiny side of one feather facing the shiny side of the other feather. This positioning will make the feathers flare away from each other. The beginning of the fibers on each quill butt section will be adjacent to each other. PHOTO 116 shows the feathers in proper alignment held in the left hand prior to tying to the shank.

5. Using the left hand, place both feathers against your side of the shank, tie down and trim off butts. Note in PHOTO 116 that

approximately 1/4 inch of bare quill is exposed *above* the hook shank. This bare quill is necessary as it will allow the first spread of fibers to flare out perpendicular to the shank. If the fibers were tied in with no bare quill showing above the shank, the first turns of fiber would lay back toward the tail, a position we want to avoid on a dry fly, PHOTO 117.

116

117

6. With your hackle pliers, grasp the tip of one feather and wind it around the shank, PHOTO 118. Keep each turn of quill to the right of, and just as close as possible, to the previous turn. When another turn isn't feasible due to the short length of the remaining feather, let the pliers hang freely below the hook to maintain tension on the hackle quill. The quill should now be situated about 1/16 inch from the eye. This blank space will allow room to form the head without disturbing the hackle fibers.

118

7. With thumb and index finger of the left hand, pull as many fibers as possible to the left. Now wind the thread over the tip of the feather three or four times to secure it to the shank. These winds *must* be made to the *left* of the hackle tip and pliers to assure that the feather quill is, indeed, being secured to the shank. Pulling the fibers to the left will prevent their being tied down. Cut the feather tip right up against the shank.

8. Repeat steps six and seven with the second feather winding it directly over the winds of the first feather, and secure it to the shank as you did the first feather. If any fibers do get tied down and protrude to the right, trim them off with your scissors as close as possible to the shank.

119

9. We are now ready to tie the head. Again

pull and hold the hackle fibers to the left. While doing so, wind the thread to form a *tapered* head, PHOTO 119.

10. The hackle guard is now used. Assuming your guards consist of three different sizes, select the guard whose hole is proper for the hook you are using. In the case of the #12 hook, the guard with the smallest hole is proper. With the guard in the position shown in PHOTO 120, slip the thread through the slot, into the hole, and bring the hole to the left over the head of the fly. The weight hanging on the string will hold the guard in place, PHOTO 121.

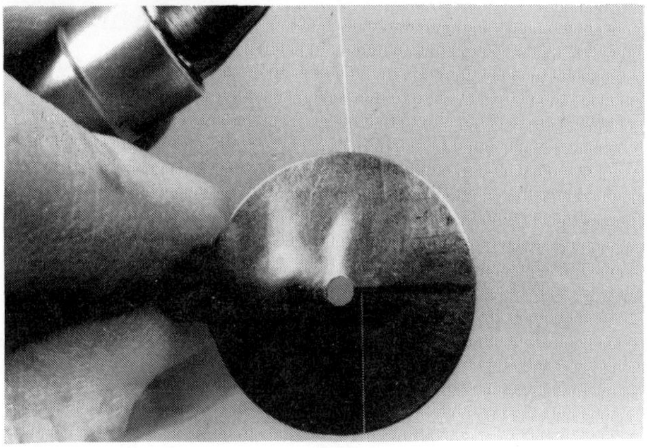

120

121

11. Tie two whip finish knots and cut the thread as close as possible to the head. The head should now be neat, relatively small, and definitely tapered.

12. With the very tip of your bodkin point, apply a neat coat of head cement completely around the head. This action is a precaution to help assure that the head doesn't unravel while in a fish's mouth.

Let me explain here the reason for tying in the two feathers with shiny side to shiny side. Just as each individual feather quill has a slight curve to it, so does each fiber on that quill. The shiny side of each feather and each fiber is the convex side. The dull side is concave. If the fibers are wound to protrude at a 90 degree angle from the shank, it is easy to see that the fibers will tend to curve either to the front or rear. In order to balance this uni-directional effect, even though it is very slight, the shiny-side-to-shiny-side technique is employed to produce fiber curves in both directions.

COLLAR HACKLE—WET FLY

The tie-in, wind, and tie-off techniques here are essentially the same as for the dry fly. Therefore, let's tie a wet fly hackle in the same manner as we did the dry hackle, but we'll incorporate the following differences:

1. Use only one feather. This feather may be taken from a wet fly neck because stiff, high-floating fibers are not wanted.

2. Tie the feather in with the shiny side *forward* so the fibers will naturally curve to the rear when wound around the shank.

3. As each wind is made, pull the fibers to the rear with your left hand. Only three or four winds are necessary as this hackle can be rather sparse.

4. Wind the feather up closer to the hook eye

than you did with the dry hackle. In so doing, you will necessarily force the fibers back as the head is formed, PHOTO 117. Because we want the fly to penetrate through the water's surface film on contact, we don't want the hackle fibers protruding 90 degrees from the shank. We want them to lay back and collapse upon meeting the water. Winding the thread *over* the fibers slightly will force them to lay back.

That's it! You now have a wet fly hackle which is more sparsely tied than the dry fly hackle, and which lays back rather than projects out at a right angle to the shank.

FORE AND AFT HACKLE

This hackle arrangement is tied either wet or dry. The characteristics of each, as explained above, apply. For the dry fly, only one good feather is necessary at each location rather than two. The aft hackle will be tied on after the tail is in place (assuming a tail is used), but before the body is wound. The technique used for the forward hackle is the same as described in the sections on "Collar Hackle—Dry Fly" and "Collar Hackle—Wet Fly."

THE PALMERED HACKLE

The Woolly Worm and Woolly Bugger patterns most commonly utilize the palmered hackle. It is wound the entire length of the body, being spiraled from the tail to the head. For our first practice hackle, let's tie it over a chenille body, which is standard on the Woolly Worm.

1. With a tail in place on a #8 hook, #79580, tie in the *tip* of a long neck or saddle hackle feather. Trim away the excess tip. Now simultaneously tie in a six inch section each of tinsel and chenille. Set the tinsel and feather back into your material clip.

2. After bringing the thread forward, wind the chenille forward to form the body, leaving enough room behind the eye for the tapered head. Secure the chenille to the shank.

3. Wind the tinsel forward creating a ribbed effect and secure it to the shank.

4. Using the right hand, grasp the butt of the hackle feather and pull it upwards until tight. Moisten the tips of the left thumb and index finger and dress *all* fibers to the left so that those fibers on the right side of the quill double back over and point in the same direction as those on the left side, PHOTO 122. Now as the feather is wound, *all* fibers will point *away* from the fly body.

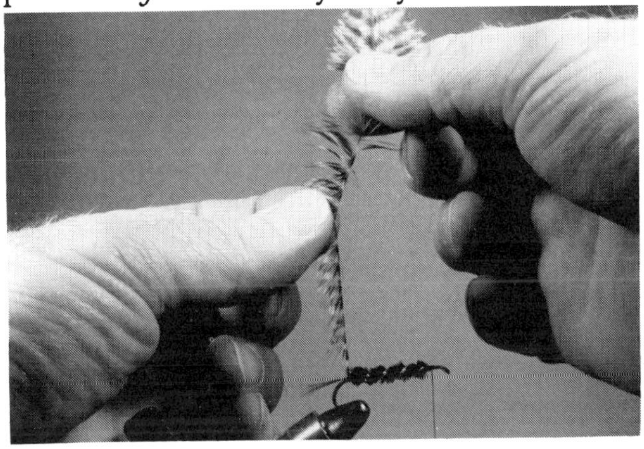

122

5. Wind the feather forward taking each turn *between* the turns of tinsel, PHOTO 123. You now have a hackle with its largest fiber length at the front of the body. Tie off, form the tapered head and whip finish, PHOTO 124. The tinsel rib is not essential, but is customary on Woolly Worm patterns.

123

124

Another technique for palmer hackles is to strip the fibers from one side of two long feathers. These are then tied in just as we did the single feather, but secured so the stripped side of the quill will wind against the body chenille, PHOTO 125. If a more sparse hackle is desired here, use only one feather.

125

THE BI-VISIBLE HACKLE

The bi-visible pattern is essentially an all-hackle fly. With the tail in place, the entire shank is wound with hackle feathers, and the last feather wound next to the eye is a white or cream color. This last feather is known as a "face" hackle, and makes the fly more visible on the water.

The procedure for tying is quite simple. Starting at the tail you tie in two or three hackle feathers as you did with the collar hackle, wind forward individually and tie off. Keep these turns compacted tightly next to each other. Now tie in two or three more hackles and repeat the process. When the shank has been covered, with room left for only one or two more hackles at the head, the next feather(s) wound (the face hackle) will be of a lighter color than the rest of the body hackles, PHOTO 126. The body hackles are usually of one color only, but mixing of colors is optional.

126

THE PARACHUTE HACKLE

A different concept is evident in the tying of this hackle type. Rather than having only the tips of the hackle fibers resting on the water, the entire length of the fiber supports the fly.

The first photo of this section illustrates the feather of the parachute hackle tied around a deer hair "post" wing, PHOTO 127. Although this is probably the most common method of tying this hackle, it is sometimes tied around a short section of the hackle feather quill, which has been bent, looped and secured at a right angle upward from the shank, PHOTO 128.

127

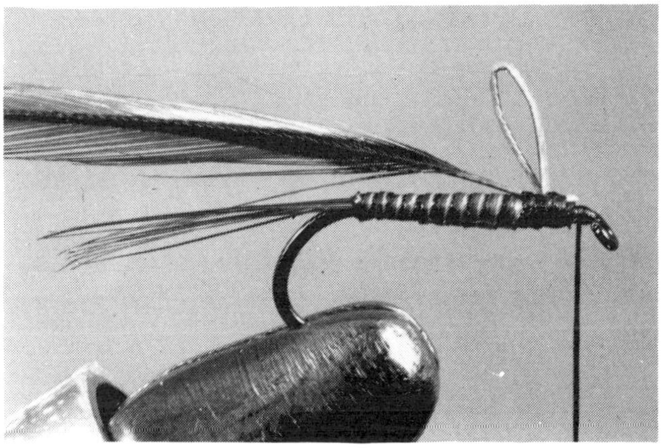

128

For your first attempt at this hackle, you'll tie it around the quill butt. After learning to tie wings, you may utilize the post wing.

1. Prepare one feather just as you did for the collar hackle. For this particular tie, the fiber length may be a bit longer than the hackle gauge would normally dictate.

2. After winding a body on the shank of a #12 dry fly hook, lay the feather lengthwise along the top of the body with the dull side down, the feather tip pointing to your left and tie down the bare quill at the front of the body. Allow at least 1/2 inch of bare quill stub to remain extended to the right of the tie-down. This extended stub section will now be bent up into a loop perpendicular to the shank and secured with winds of thread over the quill stub on the front side of the loop, toward the hook eye, PHOTO 128.

3. Grip the tip of the feather with your hackle pliers and wind counter-clockwise (viewed from above) around the loop. The first few winds should rise quickly up from the shank about 1/8 inch. The remainder of winds should then be wound back down to the shank beneath the first few winds, tied off with thread, and the feather tip cut off, PHOTO 129. As a precaution to help prevent the hackle from unwinding, a drop of cement should always be placed over the quill post to bind the turns of hackle quill to the post.

129

This method of tying the parachute hackle, tying it around its own quill, would normally be used only with spent wings, those which lay out to each side of the fly rather than standing upright. In most cases, however, this hackle will be wound around the base of an upright wing.

THROAT HACKLE

This hackle is used only on wet flies and is often referred to as a beard hackle. It is used for the representation of insect legs, or as a throat color in the case of small fish representations.

The throat hackle is tied only on the underside, and usually at the eye, of the hook. In both the insect and the fish imitations, the fibers either flare or are actually divided to lay back on both sides of the shank. We'll tie a flared, hackle fiber beard first.

1. With the tail and body in place, and the thread hanging from the front of the body, remove the hook from the vise and replace it upside-down. Pull a large hackle feather from a neck and with your scissors cut the quill at the midway point between its tip and butt. Set the feather on the top surface of the shank (actually this is now the underside of the fly body) with the tip end to your left and the dull side facing the hook. Make three winds of thread to secure the feather, PHOTO 130.

130

2. With the bobbin hanging taut, pull the feather to your right so the cut quill slips beyond the turns of thread, leaving only the fibers of the feather secured to the shank, PHOTO 131.

131

3. Additional turns of thread will now be made to permanently secure the fibers into place. At this time, the head will be formed and finished.

For our second beard, let's tie one using a partridge body feather in the divided style. Grouse or other similar feather may be used if partridge is not available.

1. Start this tie with the hook in the vise in the inverted position, with a fur body in place, as above.

2. Prepare the partridge fibers by grasping as many as possible from the left side of the feather, PHOTO 132. Remove the fibers by pulling briskly upward on the feather tip, just as you do when obtaining hackle fibers for a tail.

132

3. Transfer the fibers to your right hand,

grasping them by the butts. Set these fibers down on the hook so the fiber tips extend back even with the hook point. Re-grasp the fibers with the left hand. You can now wind the thread two or three turns to hold the fibers in place, PHOTO 133.

133

4. With your scissor points, divide the bundle of fibers into two closely equal parts. Push one section to the far side of the body and hold in place with the index finger of your left hand. Pull the other section to your side of the hook and hold it down with your left thumb, PHOTO 134.

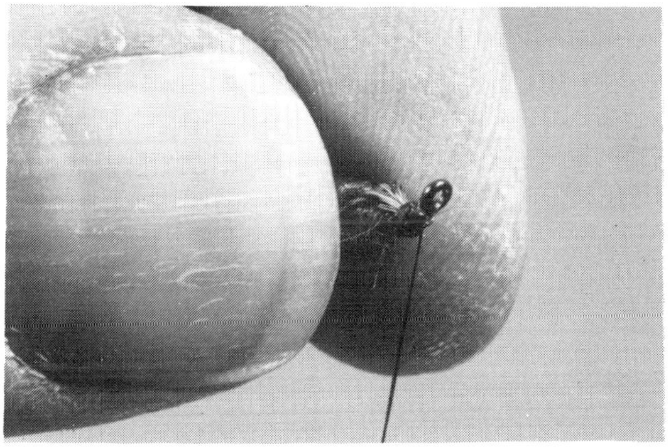

134

5. While holding these two bundles of fibers in this divided position, wind the thread to your *left* slightly over the separated sections. These winds will hold the fibers in a permanently divided position to represent the legs coming from each side of the insect's body, PHOTO 135.

135

6. Form the head, whip finish, and cement.

The hackle types described in this chapter represent situations you will encounter in the tying of 95% of your flies. Variations of these techniques do of course exist, but with the skills you now have, tying these variations should not prove difficult. The procedure for winding dry fly hackles with the wings already in place is described on page 88.

We have now come to the exploration of the final major part of the dry fly—the wings. Although we are learning the wings as the last of the major fly elements, the wings of the dry fly are, in fact, almost always tied on before the other elements.

Throughout this chapter we'll examine the materials and the techniques which will enable you to tie almost all winged dry fly patterns in use today. Hopefully during the time between my writing and your reading this chapter, new ideas will have developed which both of us can enjoy learning.

Nymph patterns do not have wings. Dry flies, streamers and traditional wet flies usually do have wings. This chapter will be relatively long in order to expose you to the several variations of wing types. Many of the wings you will learn utilize the same *basic* tying techniques, but with slight modifications to accommodate the material used or the representation desired.

At this stage of your tying proficiency, you should have developed reasonably good control of the thread-winding with your right hand, and have developed a fair talent for holding and placing materials with your left hand. Both of these skills will be further tested and tuned as we proceed through this chapter.

DRY FLY WINGS—GENERAL DISCUSSION

The first few wings you'll learn are referred to as "upright and divided." These are the wings we see on the classic dry fly patterns in catalogs and display counters. They represent wings of the natural, adult mayfly while he spends his brief time span alive in the atmosphere. When he dies, his wings collapse and become "spent" wings, which we'll discuss later.

The upright and divided wings may be tied with a variety of materials, but they all have the same following characteristics:

1. They are two gaps long.

2. They are secured directly on top of the hook shank.

3. They are tied onto a base of thread.

4. They are set perpendicular to the shank.

5. They are tied in at a point approximately 1/4 to 1/3 shank length back from the hook eye.

HACKLE TIP WINGS

This wing is tied using the tips of two hackle feathers. The feathers are taken from about the same place on the neck from which we would select the hackle feathers for the size hook we are dressing. The tying procedure is as follows:

1. Lay down a base of thread on the shank of a #12 dry fly hook at the wing location and let the thread hang from the center of this base, PHOTO 136.

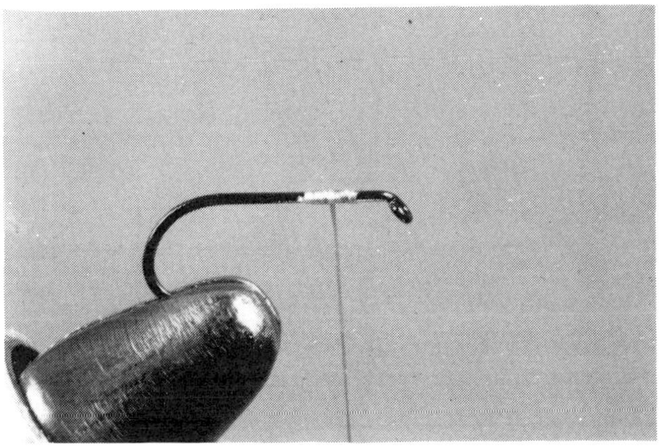

136

2. With the left hand hold two hackle feathers, shiny side to shiny side, tips pointing to the right, with slightly less than two gaps distance between the end of your thumb and the end of the feathers, PHOTO 137.

3. Hold the feathers about 1/8 inch above the shank, bring the thread straight up and pinch, wind around 360 degrees and pinch again, and pull the thread straight up to tighten the loop. This is the identical tie-in process we used on the tail. Remember? Now wind the thread five or six times to the left to secure the feathers tightly to the shank. They should be two gaps long from tie-down to tips. Trim off the butts of the feathers, PHOTO 138.

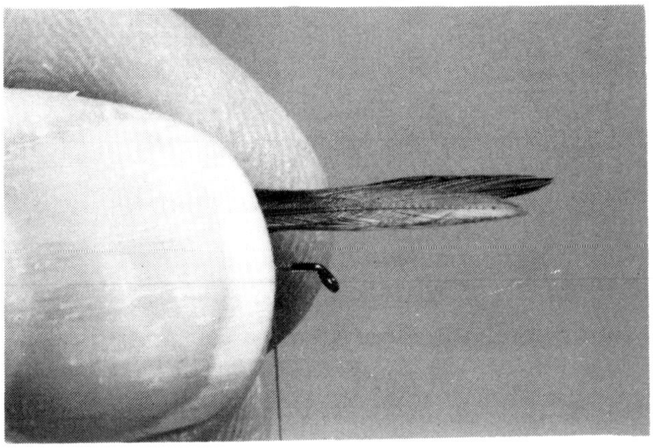

137

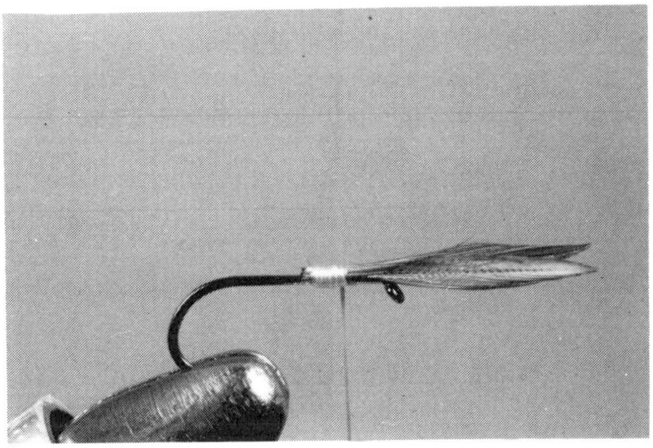

138

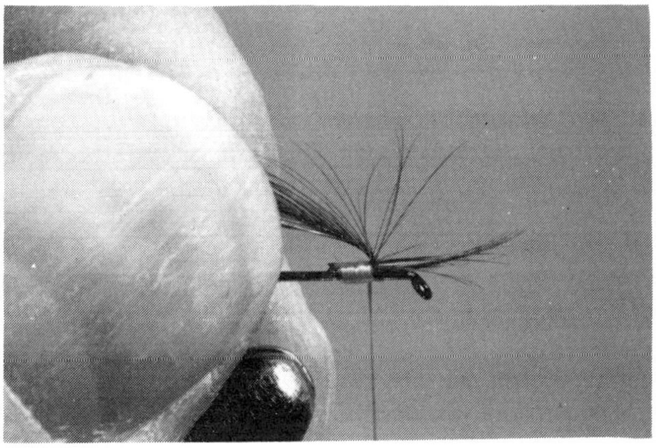

139

4. You must now make the hackle tips stand straight upright. To do this, you pull the two wings back to the left beyond the vertical position. Allow those fibers which will, to fall to the right, PHOTO 139.

5. Now wind your thread around the shank immediately in front of, and touching, the quills. This "wedge" will force the feathers to remain upright. You should now trim off those short fibers protruding to the right. Now half of our upright and divided requirement has been satisfied, PHOTO 140. The next step is to secure the feathers into a permanently divided position. If your wings have rolled around slightly to the far side of the shank during steps three, four, and five, merely pinch the base of the wings with your tweezers and roll them back to their proper position on top of the shank.

140

6. You'll now do a "figure 8" with the tying thread. This procedure will involve criss-crossing the thread between the wings to separate and hold them permanently in the divided position. Here's the way it works. With your left hand grasp the feather tip closest to you (the near feather). Wind the thread up to vertical above the hook, bring it back to the left between the wings, PHOTO 141, and wind it down so the thread is now taut below the shank. All you have done is taken just one wind of thread around the shank, but you placed it *between* the wings.

141

7. Now with your left hand, hold the tip of the far wing, bring the thread up to vertical and this time bring the thread *forward* between the wings, PHOTO 142. You have just completed a "figure 8." It's very important throughout this process to keep the thread very close to the base of the wing quills. In other words, don't let the thread wander along the shank forward or back of the quills because this will result in too great an angle of approach between the wings and will push the wings out of proper alignment. It is also important to hold each wing in a relatively vertical position while executing the figure 8 to prevent the wing from being set at an angle too far down toward the horizontal plane.

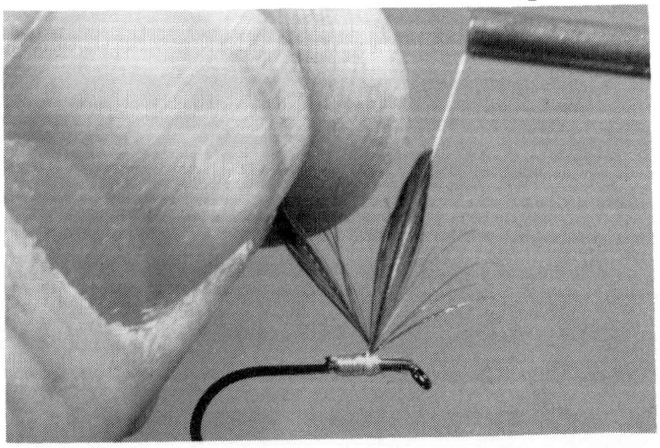

142

8. When the wing is complete, the thread is wound back into position for tying in the tail, PHOTO 143.

143

As mentioned in step seven, thread location is extremely important when manipulating wings into proper position. A 1/50th of an inch can dictate success or failure, so keep the thread in tight near the quills!

Should one wing or the other want to lean forward or back, merely complete a full or half figure 8 putting the thread in front of the wing you wish to push back and behind the wing you wish to push forward. The thread merely has to touch the quill to change its position. These are subtle maneuvers and must be practiced thoroughly to be mastered.

You have just learned several basic fundamentals in the tying of wings. For the different styles and materials to be learned hereafter, I will refer to the terminology just used for the hackle tip wing without discussing the procedure in great detail. For this reason, I suggest you *practice*! Don't tie one example of each style and tell yourself you have it mastered. It doesn't come that easily! Practice makes tying easier, quicker and more consistent.

ROLLED WINGS

Only one feather is required for this wing, even though it does have a divided configuration. The feather involved is the flank feather from a woodduck and is many times referred to in pattern descriptions merely as "woodduck" or "lemon woodduck." The flank feather from a Mandarin duck may also be used as it is essentially identical to the woodduck.

Because the supply of these feathers is limited, the cost is relatively high and exceeds what many people are willing to pay. For this reason, a reasonably priced substitute is available in the form of dyed mallard duck breast feathers.

Although their tying performance is not as high as the woodduck, we'll use the mallard feather to learn the tying procedure. In the future, when you use a woodduck feather, you'll appreciate the difference! In either case the process is identical.

1. The fibers in the tip of the feather are those which will comprise the wings. You'll tie them in, tie them up to vertical, and divide them. One problem can occur because you're forming two wings with a feather which contains only one quill. If the quill should become part of one wing only, the fly will be unbalanced. Therefore, the quill must be removed *if* it would extend up far enough to become part of one wing or the other. I'll explain!

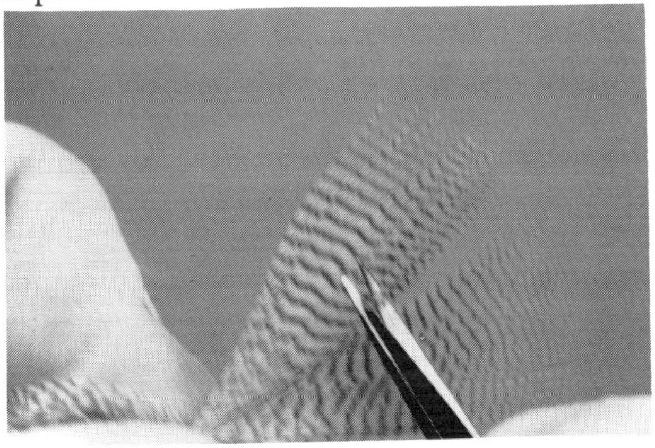

144

2. Hold the feather in front of you. Estimate the length of two gaps for the hook size on

which you are tying. Mentally or physically measure this two gap distance from the tip of the feather toward the butt. If the *quill* itself extends up into this two gap distance, that portion of the quill will have to be removed. This is simply done by cutting the quill with your scissor points below the two gap distance, PHOTO 144.

3. Hold the fibers of the tip of the feather with your left thumb and index finger, estimating the two gap length which will become the wing, as you did with the hackle tips. Tie them down firmly onto your base of thread, trim the butts, and wedge to upright, just as you did with the hackle tips. The only difference will be the need to wind *more* of a wedge to keep the fibers vertical, PHOTO 145.

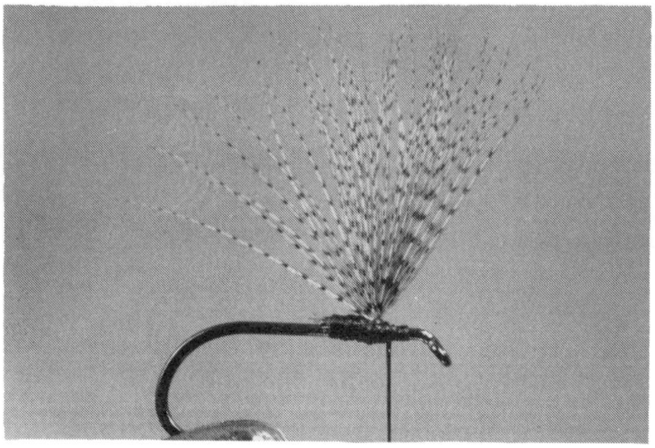

145

4. Sometimes at this stage of tying the wing, the fibers flare excessively. If they do, we can compact them by winding the thread 360 degrees around the total bundle of fibers, not around the shank, but above it. The thread is *not* wound around the shank itself, only around the fibers, PHOTO 146. You now have a post wing as mentioned when we discussed the parachute hackle!

5. You must now divide the bundle of fibers into two closely equal sections. If you are tying with the scissors in your hand, as you should be, use the points to divide the bundle, PHOTO 147. Hold the near wing and wind the thread between the wings in a figure 8. Continue with the figure 8 as you did with the hackle tip wings until they remain upright and divided.

146

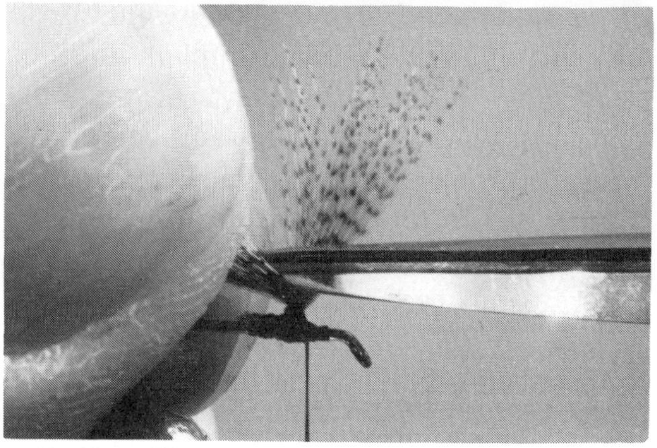

147

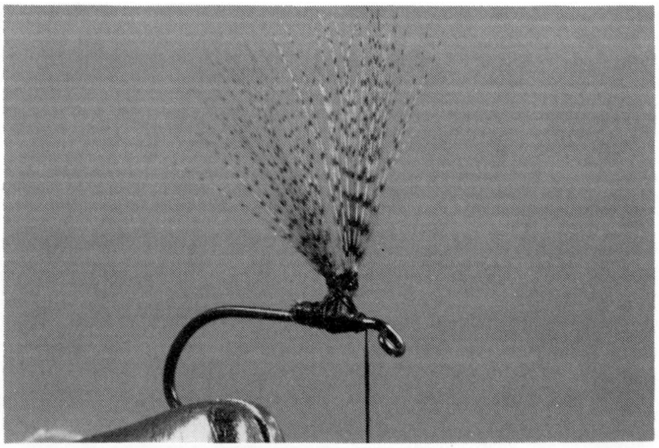

148

6. One more step may be required with this wing. After step five, the two bundles might be too flared and fluffy, as was the initial

single bundle. If we again wish to tighten up the base of the wings to correct some of the flare, a 360 degree wind around each wing individually is required. PHOTO 148 shows with exaggerated thread the pattern taken around the wings by the thread. As these turns are made, the wing being encircled should be held upright with the left hand to prevent lateral movement of the wing.

DUCK OR GOOSE QUILL WINGS

The tying procedure for quill wings is very similar to that of the hackle tips. Two separate pieces of material are used, and put into the upright and divided position.

For our practice here, we'll use mallard duck wing primary feathers. The primaries are the longer feathers from the front edge of the wing. A pair of feathers is required. This does not mean merely two feathers, but rather closely corresponding feathers from both the left and the right wings. When compared to each other the feathers bend in opposite directions and present a mirror image, PHOTO 149. Two feathers from the same duck wing will not work for the artificial fly wings. A pair of duck wings (or primary quills) is required and should be purchased as such.

149

1. Our first step is to cut a quill section from the wide side of each feather. These sections will be of the same width, PHOTO 150, approximately 3/16 inch for a #12 hook.

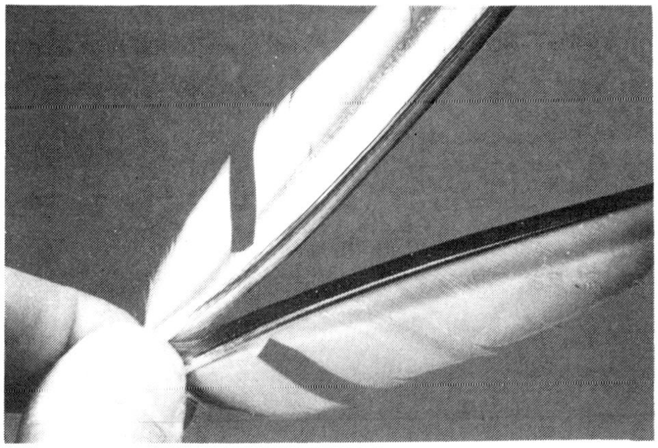

150

2. With the sections curving away from each other, shiny side to shiny side, hold the sections so the *points* of each quill section are facing downward, PHOTO 151.

151

152

3. Set the quills down *near* the base of the

thread and tie in just as you did with the hackle tip wings. When the quills are in their upright and divided position, apply a thin coat of head cement to their points to help prevent their splitting when in use, PHOTO 152.

Even with the precaution of using the cement, the wings will split and look ragged after the fly has been fished for a while.

DEER HAIR WINGS

The fibers of deer hair in a wing have the same floating quality as those used in the deer hair tail and body. Therefore, it's a very desirable material to use in flies which will be fished on rough water. These wings are tied from deer body hair and the procedure is very similar to the rolled wing.

1. Cut about 40 hairs from the deer skin. Pluck or comb out the underfur, and even the tips, as you did for the deer hair tail using either the fingers and palm method or using a hair stacker.

2. A strong thread should be used with this wing because a good deal of pressure is required to hold the hair in place. Use a #8 hook, and on a base of thread, tie down the hair bundle as you did the rolled wing. Wind firmly to prevent the bundle from rolling around the shank, PHOTO 153. A drop of cement under the bundle will help a great deal to prevent the bundle from rolling when the fly is being fished.

3. Lift the bundle, wedge it into a permanent upright position, and divide with figure 8's and 360's. The wing is now complete. Wind the thread to the rear and you're ready to tie in the tail. Most commonly the tail is also tied with deer hair, although moose body hair will work well also.

153

154

155

When tied in *first*, these wings will be used in conjunction with a body material *other than* deer hair. When tied with a clipped deer hair body, these wings are tied in *after* the body is complete. Merely tie in as usual immediately in front of the body, PHOTO 154. To complete, bring upright and divide, PHOTO 155. Trim the butts so they become part of the body.

FOLD-OVER HAIR BACKSTRAP AND WING COMBINATION

The application of deer hair over the body of the fly pattern called the Goofus Bug (also referred to as the Humpy) offers the advantage of good floatability along with ease of tying. The hair is neither spun nor clipped, but merely folded over the top of the body to form a "hump." This particular dressing is interesting, however, in that we use this same "hump" hair bundle to form the wings. The procedure goes like this:

1. Tie in a deer hair tail as usual, two gaps long.

2. Now tie in another bundle of deer hair resembling a tail, but its length must be two gaps *plus* the body length. This bundle will be tied down at the same point at which the tail is tied down, PHOTO 156. Make sure you have also evened the tips of this latter bundle.

156

3. Wind a floss body and allow the thread to hang at the front of the body.

4. With your right hand, pull the second hair bundle to your right over the top of the body. Make sure all of the hairs are pulled tightly forward, PHOTO 157.

157

5. With your left hand take several winds of thread around the hair and shank to hold it firmly in position. You have now formed the hump and should take a few more winds of thread with your right hand to permanently secure the bundle in place, PHOTO 158.

158

6. The hair tips now protruding to your right are the wings. With your left hand, pull these hairs upright and wedge them. The balance of the procedure is identical to tying the upright and divided deer hair wing.

KIP TAIL WINGS

The hair from the tail of a calf is used for

this wing. The hair is also called "calf tail" and "impala." Normally the wing is tied with natural white, but this hair is dyed many colors for many different applications.

It is tied in the same manner as the deer hair wing with the exception of the method used to even the hair tips. These calf tail hairs are crinkly and less stiff than are the deer hairs, therefore they won't slide in the crease of the finger nor do they tamp down well when put into a hair stacking tool.

1. Clip a bundle of hair from the tail and hold it by the butts with your right hand. With your left hand, pull out the longest hairs and lay them back into the main bundle so the tips are even with the hairs in the bundle, PHOTO 159. Repeat the process if necessary until all of the hair tips to be used in the wing are approximately even, PHOTO 160.

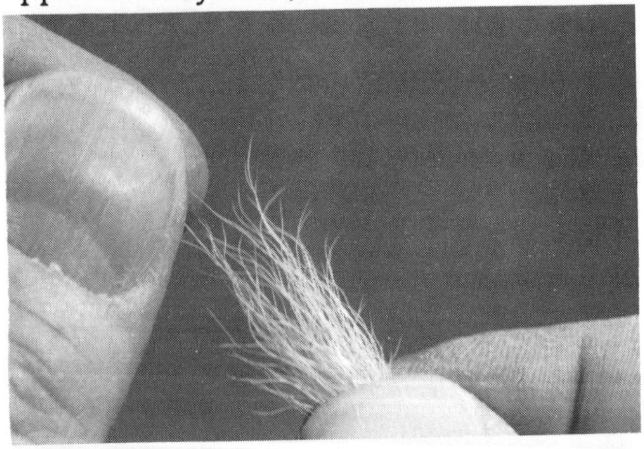

159

160

2. Secure the hairs to a #8 hook, bring upright, do a 360 wind, figure 8 to divide, do the 360's around each wing, and take the thread back into position to tie in the tail. This procedure is done the same way you did the deer hair. PHOTO 161 illustrates the complete wing. For added durability you may wish to set this wing into a drop of head cement applied to the base thread.

161

YARN WINGS

This is a less often used wing, but one which has merit and will probably continue to gain in popularity. It is tied using polypropylene yarn and has the advantages of being non-water absorbant, very light in weight, translucent, and can be cut to any shape desired. On the negative side of the scale is the relative difficulty encountered in getting the wings to look as nice as you think they should look. We'll tie both a divided and a single wing type.

A - DIVIDED POLY WINGS

1. Use a section of poly yarn about two inches long. If the yarn is essentially round in cross section at this stage, stroke it lengthwise to make it wider and flatter.

2. Fold the yarn into a loop two gaps long, flat side to flat side. Hold the loop slightly above the shank with the loop out over the eye of the hook, PHOTO 162. Tie the loop down firmly, pull to your left, and secure in the vertical position, PHOTO 163. Cut the tip of the loop to form two wings, and figure 8 to divide into two separate wings.

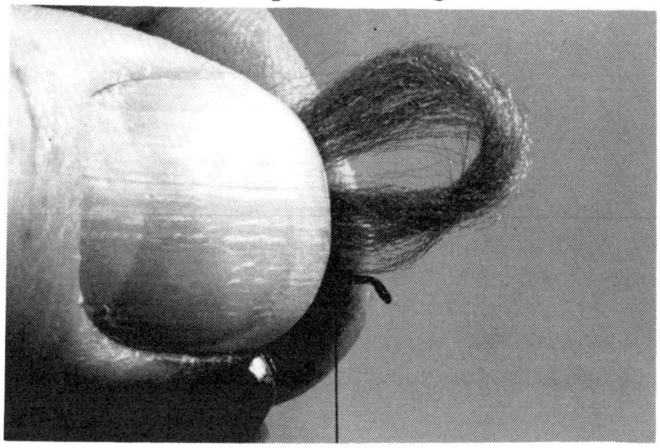

162

163

164

3. The wings should then be trimmed to shape, with the front edge more to vertical (when viewed from the side), and the rear edge sloped back, PHOTO 164, as are the wings of the natural mayfly.

B - SINGLE POLY WING

1. Repeat step one above.

2. Fold a loop as above except this time form the loop with the *edges* together rather than the flats, PHOTO 165. Tie in perpendicular to the shank, with the four edges facing to the front and rear. In other words, tie in so you are looking at a wide, flat wing, PHOTO 166. There is no need to divide or figure 8 this wing.

165

166

3. Now cut the top of the loop and shape a wing which slopes to the rear, PHOTO 167.

This makes a perfect type wing around which you can wind a parachute hackle.

167

SPENT WINGS

With the poly wing we've concluded the tying of upright and divided wings. Before we proceed to what we call downwings, I want to discuss the spent wing. This style lies flat on the water representing the natural wing of the dead adult mayfly. We'll review the three different ties of this wing most commonly used.

168

A - SPENT WINGS—HACKLE TIP

The most effective method of tying this style is to first tie the wings upright and divided as you did in the section on "The Hackle Tip Wings." The rest is easy. Merely pull the near wing down to the horizontal, PHOTO 168 and figure 8. Then hold the far wing down and figure 8 again, PHOTO 169. This process may require a repeat to set them permanently into the spent position, but usually two or three figure 8's will get the job done.

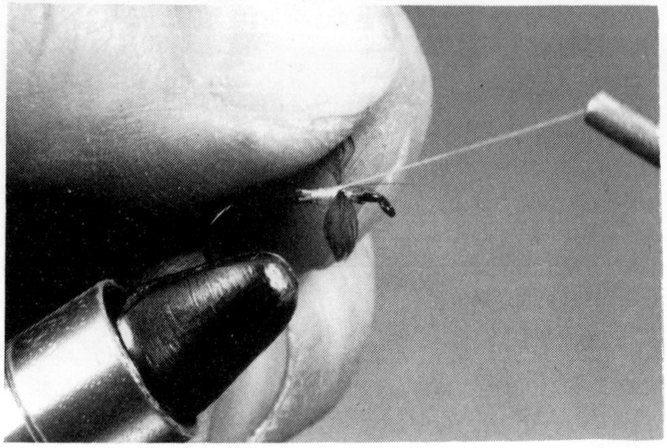

169

B - SPENT WINGS—HAIR TYPE

Although part of the function of a spent wing is to assist the fly to float, the hair wing normally is not tied with deer hair, the main reason being the excessive flare cause by the thread when it's tied in.

The hair most commonly used is a good stiff hair whose tips can be easily evened. One I particularly like is that from a mink tail. A similar, but slightly more delicate, wing can be tied of hackle fibers. These fibers will look just like the hackle fiber tail but will extend perpendicular to both sides of the shank at the wing location. We'll use the hackle fibers for practice, but keep in mind that the mink, or other tail hairs, would be tied in an identical manner.

1. After winding a base of thread, grasp about two dozen fibers from the left side of a large hackle feather just as you do the dozen fibers for the tail.

2. Hold the fibers above the shank with the tips pointing out over the eye of the hook two

gaps long from the point of tie-down; just as you did the deer hair wing. Tie down securely and trim off the butts, PHOTO 170.

170

3. With your scissor points, divide the fibers into two bundles. Pull the near bundle toward you with your left hand and wind thread around the shank in front of this bundle in one-half of a figure 8 style until it stands out relatively perpendicular to the shank in a horizontal plane, PHOTO 171.

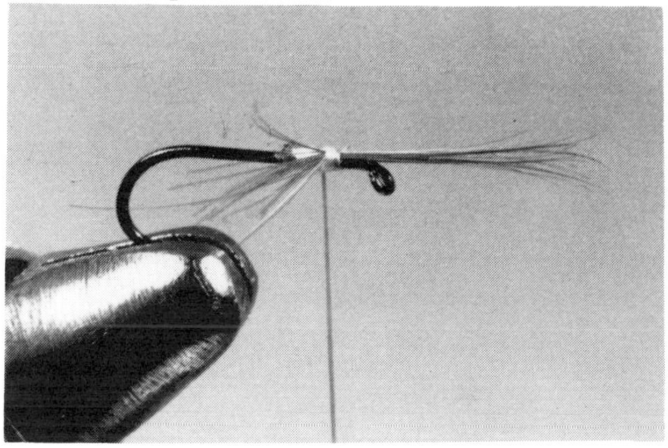

171

4. Pull the far bundle away from you and wind the thread around the shank in front of this bundle, again in one-half of a figure 8 fashion.

5. Now do normal figure 8's until both wings are in a horizontal plane and perpendicular to the shank, PHOTO 172.

172

C - SPENT WINGS—POLYPROPYLENE YARN

This wing uses the same yarn material as the poly upright wing and the procedure for tying it is very simple.

1. Cut a one inch section of poly yarn and flatten it out as you did for the upright wing.

2. On a base of thread, lay the yarn section horizontally across the hook shank at a right angle to the shank. Tie down with figure 8's to hold in position. Round off the wing tips as desired, PHOTO 173.

173

DOWNWINGS—GENERAL DISCUSSION

There are several materials used to tie

wings in the down position. These materials and this wing style are used to represent either the wings of insects whose natural wings lay back flat over their bodies, or they represent the total body of a small fish.

On the pages to follow in this chapter, you'll learn the various downwings for tying several insect and minnow imitations.

We'll start with a basic flat quill wing. Such a wing might be used in representing a beetle or adult caddis fly. A feather from the wing of most any bird can be used depending on the color and texture desired. Should the color preferred not be available in the natural wing, the quill can be lacquered the desired shade or colored with a permanent ink, felt-tipped marking pen.

A - FLAT QUILL SECTION WING

1. For our example here, we'll use a section from a duck wing feather. On a #12 dry fly hook, palmer a hackle over a dubbed fur body. With your scissors, trim out the top and bottom fibers allowing the hackle to extend only to both sides of the shank, PHOTO 174.

174

2. Cut a quill section about 3/16 inch wide from the duck feather.

3. With the tip end of this quill held between your left thumb and index finger, set the section on the hook shank and tie down at the front of the hackle. Trim off excess quill and finish head, PHOTO 175.

175

4. Now the quill section should be "feather-glazed" as you also cement the head. This process involves applying a thin coat of head cement to the quill with the tip of your bodkin. It adds strength to the quill and helps prevent splitting. Round off the square corners on the tip end of the wing, PHOTO 176.

176

B - FLAT BODY-FEATHER WING

This wing is very similar in appearance to the quill wing but utilizes a bird body feather rather than a wing feather. We'll use a partridge feather for this example.

1. As for the preparation of the hook prior to tying in this wing, we can use the same body/hackle arrangement used on the previous quill wing.

2. Have a partridge feather ready on the tying table and apply a couple drops of head cement to the tips of the thumb and index finger of your left hand.

3. Lay the feather between these two fingers and stroke it with the cement to glaze both sides, PHOTO 177. The tighter you squeeze the feather the narrower in width it becomes, so you have the ability to size the feather to match the size of the hook on which you are tying. While pulling on the feather with the proper pressure to result in the width you desire, blow on it a couple of times to dry the cement. The feather preparation is now complete.

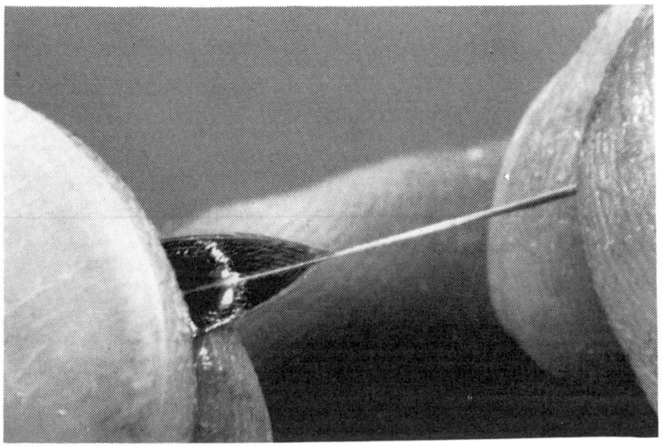

177

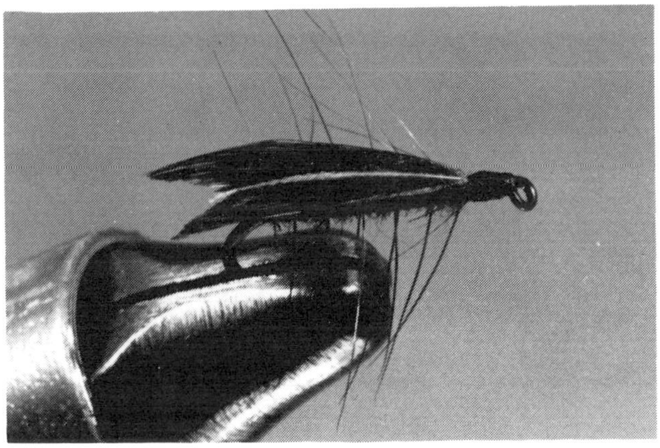

178

4. The next, and last, step is merely to lay the feather, concave side down, across the top of the body and tie down at the head, PHOTO 178. If you wish to shape the rear end of the wing, this can easily be done with your scissors.

C - DOWNWING—HACKLE FIBER

The technique here has become a familiar style of tying the wing representation for the adult caddisfly. The method of material application is essentially identical to the tying of the hackle fiber tail.

1. From a large hackle neck or saddle feather, pinch a bundle of fibers from the quill. Set the bundle down on top of the shank, tips to the left, at the desired length (usually with the tips at or slightly beyond the hook bend) and tie the fibers down in front of the body, PHOTO 179. If a denser wing is desired, tie in another bundle.

179

2. A wing of this type, used in the representation of adult caddis and stoneflies, is normally followed by the application of a collar hackle in front of the wing, PHOTO 180.

180

D - DOWNWING—ELK HAIR

This wing is most frequently associated with a fly named the Elk Hair Caddis, an extremely popular floating representation of the adult caddisfly. It utilizes the hair of an elk, but the tying technique is the same as that of the deer hair tail except the hair is tied in at the front of the body in the manner described above for the hackle fiber downwing. The elk hair flares more than the hackle fibers, its bulk gives a wider, denser silhouette to the artificial, and the hollow elk hairs provide excellent floatability.

This wing can be tied in conjunction with a collar hackle as indicated for the hackle fiber wing, but it often is tied without a hackle. In this case, the stub ends of the elk hair are not trimmed close to the hook shank and covered with the head, but rather are trimmed to extend out over the eye of the hook, and the whip finish knot is tied at the hook eye under the hair stubs. PHOTO 184, although not a caddis imitation, illustrates this treatment of leaving the hair over the eye.

E - DOWNWING—HACKLE WEB

The wing structure here is one I developed to more closely represent the actual silhouette of adult caddis, stonefly and midge flies. The caddis and stonefly imitations require two wings and the midge only one.

This type of dressing provides us the opportunity to tie a wing more realistic in appearance than the hair or fiber wings and it is less susceptible to fraying and splitting than the quill or body feather wings you've already tied. For your practice here, I'll describe the two-wing procedure. We'll tie a caddis on a #12 dry fly hook.

1. Start with a body of dubbed fur and a palmered hackle, cut out on top. Select two large feathers from a hackle neck. With the tip of one feather in your left hand, grasp the feather at about midpoint or lower on the quill, and pull the fibers down toward the butt forming a tight formation of fibers along each side of the quill. This resulting webby-looking formation is the first of the two wings, PHOTO 181.

181

2. With your right hand, set the formation down on top of the shank at a slight offset to the far side rather than directly down on top of the body. Tie down by winding the thread with your left hand, PHOTO 182. Trim off all excess material extending out over the eye of the hook.

182

3. Repeat the previous steps and set the second wing slightly offset to the near side of the body. *Don't* trim away the excess quite yet.

4. If you wish to have antennae on the fly, trim off all but two of the fibers now extending

to the right. Let these fibers curve to either side of the eye and, as you wind the head, figure 8 between the fibers to assure they remain separated, PHOTO 183.

183

5. To add durability to the wings, coat them with a glaze of cement.

F - DOWNWING—BUCKTAIL STREAMER

Many artificial imitations of small fish, whether for fresh or salt water fishing, utilize the hair from the tail of a deer. This hair is either white or brown in its natural state or dyed a myriad of bright colors either to represent bait fish or merely to act as an attractor lure to get the fish's attention. Other hair, such as kip tail or squirrel tail, is also commonly used.

The most popular freshwater hook used for bucktails is a Mustad #79580. This shank is 4 extra long and permits a good representation of the long, slender silhouette peculiar to most bait fish.

1. For purposes of practicing this wing, merely wind a chenille body from the tail to near the head. For the photographs, I have used a #2 hook. Add a beard hackle to the body.

2. From a piece of bucktail, cut a bundle of hair. It is neither necessary nor desirable to even the tips of the hair. Obviously if a hair or two is exceptionally long relative to the rest of the bundle, pull it out and discard, but the remainder of hairs can taper naturally to somewhat of a point when held together.

3. Hold the bundle above the shank and tie down at the point which will be the *rear* of the finished head, PHOTO 184. For added durability, I'd place a drop of head cement on the shank at this tie-down location and tie the hair into the cement.

184

4. The butt ends of hair must now be trimmed away. Rather than holding the scissors to cut the hairs at a 90 degree angle to the shank, which would result in a very blunt vertical cut-off, hold the scissors at an angle which will effect a tapered cut as in PHOTO 185. This trimming action will greatly facilitate the forming of a nicely tapered head.

185

5. Before winding the head to conclude the fly, it is usually helpful to first take a couple of 360's around the *hair only* immediately behind the head, PHOTO 186. The purpose of this action is to help compact the wing, and prevent its flaring and rolling over to the side of the shank.

186

6. To finish the fly, make several winds of thread over the hair butts to form a solid, tapered head, PHOTO 187. On flies of this size, two applications of cement are recommended to assure a firm, durable head.

187

This same procedure would be used if you tied the wing using other types of hair fibers.

G - DOWNWING–THE HACKLE FEATHER STREAMER

As with the bucktail patterns, the feather streamer also represents a small fish. Instead of hair fibers being used as the wing over the body, long neck hackle or saddle hackle feathers are used. The procedure in tying is as follows:

1. Place into your vise the same type hook, body and beard you used for the bucktail. Remove four long feathers from a neck or saddle skin. The neck hackles are usually preferred as they are normally greater in width (longer fibers) than the saddle feathers.

2. Hold one of the feathers over the top of the hook so its tip extends between one-half and one full hook length beyond the bend. This length is based on individual preference. Set your right thumb nail on the quill at the front of the body, PHOTO 188.

188

189

3. Cut off the quill 1/2 inch to the *right* of this thumb location and *cut* off the fibers to 1/16

inch long in this 1/2 inch section, PHOTO 189. These 1/16 inch long stubs will help prevent the quills from rolling as the wing is tied in.

4. The other three feathers should be identically cut using the first feather as a model. All four feathers are now the same in length and trim.

5. Align the four feathers as in PHOTO 190. The two near feathers have their shiny side *toward* you, and the two far feathers have their shiny sides *away* from you.

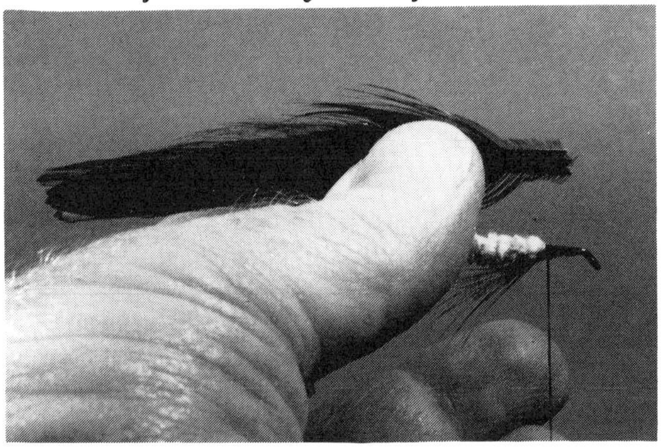

190

6. Holding all the feathers close to the trimmed butts, and at a slight upward incline to your left over the body, let the butts straddle the shank immediately in front of the body, and wind down tightly with your thread. Your wings now appear as in PHOTO 191. Finish the head to complete the fly.

191

H - DOWNWING—GRASSHOPPER STYLE

Grasshopper wings are normally tied from bird wing quill sections, are tied in separately, and are positioned along the sides of the body. The standard material for hopper wings has been quill sections from turkey wing feathers. As noted earlier, these brown feathers have become extremely rare, so substitutes are usually used. A matched pair is required.

1. For the hook, use a Mustad #94831 or a #9672, size #8. These hooks are 3xl shank to represent the long, narrow body shape of the hopper. The standard dressing calls for a red tail and yellow polypropylene yarn body over which a brown hackle has been palmered and trimmed as in the photos. Apply these to the hook.

2. Each turkey wing feather has a flat side and a curved side; which means the quill fibers extend essentially straight out from one side of the main feather stem, and somewhat curved from the other side of the stem. The fibers you are interested in are the curved ones. Before you cut out the sections to be used as wings, the feathers should be featherglazed. This can be done either by applying a thin coat of head cement to the quill with your bodkin, or spraying the feather with a lacquer-type spray material which is sold in artist supply stores to be used as a sealer over some of the materials artists put on paper.

3. Cut a section 1/4 inch wide from the curved side of each feather, PHOTO 66, page 38.

4. Select and hold one section in the left hand, with the tip pointing *up* and the concave (dull) side facing you. Set the section against the far side of the body to allow the tip

to extend back to the end of the tail. Tie this wing on first, holding the section primarily on the side of the body, but slightly up on top of the body, PHOTO 192. Tie securely into place.

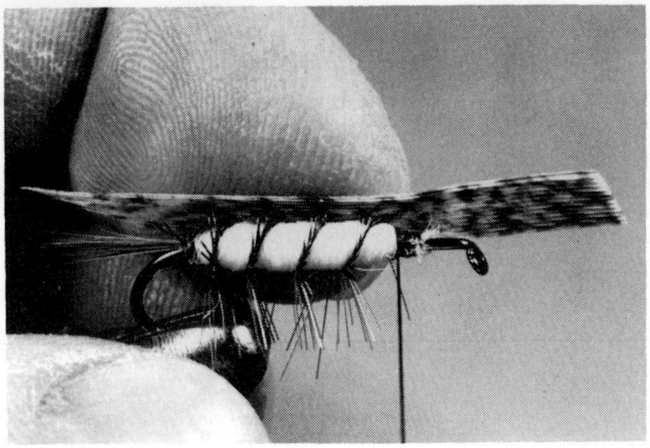

192

5. Tie in the other quill section on the near side of the body, again with the tip pointing *up*, the fibers cupping around the body, and slightly on top of the body, PHOTO 193.

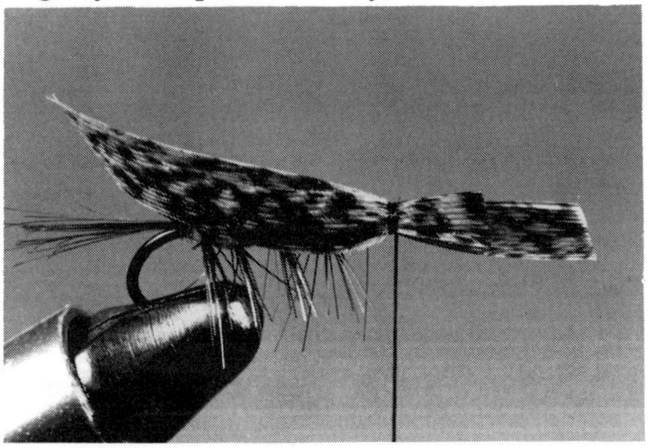

193

194

6. The last step in dressing this pattern is to wind two or three hackle feathers over the wing tie-down thread and also forward of the wings, PHOTO 194.

I - DOWNWING—SPLAYED TYPE

A splayed wing is one in which the two wings flare away from each other. The Muddler Minnow offers a good example of this wing type, and we'll use it to illustrate the procedure. Use the same hook as we did for the Grasshopper.

1. Prior to setting the wings, tie in a short tail of turkey quill, wind a body of gold tinsel and tie down an underwing of brown bear hair. This underwing acts as a base on which to tie the wings of turkey quill PHOTO 195.

195

2. As with the hopper, cut two 1/4 inch sections from the curved sides of a pair of turkey wing quills. These sections need not be featherglazed, but may be if desired.

3. Hold both sections together in the left hand, tips up, flaring away from each other, as illustrated in PHOTO 196 (held here in the right hand for clarity only).

4. Apply a drop of head cement to the top of the bear hair at the point where it is tied down, and set both quills vertically down on top of this spot. Tightly tie down both wings

onto the underwing. Trim the butts and the wing is complete, PHOTO 197.

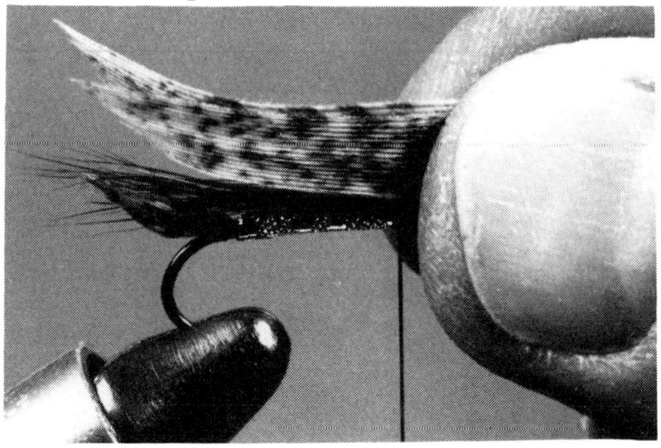

196

197

5. At this stage the deer hair hackle is tied (see Section J below) and the deer hair head is spun onto a bare shank just as you did when spinning the deer hair body. A normal thread head is whip finished and completed. The deer hair head (*not* the hackle) is trimmed to a desired shape (the photo is typical) and the fly is complete, PHOTO 198.

198

J - HACKLING WITH DEER HAIR

I intentionally omitted this hackle type from Chapter Six because I want you to tie it on the Muddler Minnow whose wings you have just completed. With the hackle explanation here, you may complete this fly.

With rare exceptions, hackles are tied using feathers. One exception does arise when tying the Muddler because the hackle on this pattern is tied with deer body hair. The hairs don't stand out perpendicular to the shank, but rather lay back in the manner of a wet fly hackle.

The application of the hairs to the shank is exactly as we applied the first bundle of hairs to form the clipped deer hair body. Remember?

1. Cut a bundle of 30 to 40 hairs from your piece of deer hide. Remove the underfur. Even-up the tips of hair.

2. With your thread still hanging from the wing tie-down, set the bundle onto the wing tie-down thread with the hair tips pointing to your left. Do *not* cut off the tips when using hair for *hackle.*

3. The hairs should be about 1/2 inch long from their tips to the point of tie-down. Distribute the hairs around the entire shank by manipulation with your fingers. You won't be able to spin this bundle of hair because it will be tied onto thread rather than the bare hook.

4. When the hairs are evenly distributed around the shank, wind the thread to secure. The butts of this hackle will be incorporated into the clipped hair head of the fly as seen in PHOTO 198.

K - HACKLING AROUND UPRIGHT WINGS

We have now separately discussed the tying of wings and the application of hackles, but it's important here to concentrate on winding the hackle when upright wings are in place. This isn't a difficult procedure, but it's necessary to know the techniques which make the hackling efficient and effective. The principles learned in the chapter on tying hackles still apply, but the tying process changes slightly because we now have the wings in place.

1. Measuring, stripping and grasping the two hackle feathers remain the same as you learned in Chapter Six.

2. With the tying thread hanging directly in front of the wings, set the bare hackle quills along your side of the hook and secure with the thread still in front of the wings. Trim away the quill butts, PHOTO 199. Remember to have about 1/4 inch of bare quill above the shank.

199

3. When you start to wind the hackle feathers, the first turns will be made *behind* the wings. It's therefore necessary to secure the two quills behind the wings by winding the thread to a position immediately behind them and making a couple of turns of thread over the bare hackle quills. When you have accomplished this, bring the thread forward again and let it hang midway between the wings and the eye of the hook, PHOTO 200.

200

201

4. You will now grasp one feather with your hackle pliers and wind two or three turns of hackle *behind* the wings, PHOTO 201. After the second or third wind, and when the feather is being held taut *beneath* the hook shank, pull the feather forward so your next wind will be in *front* of the wings. Wind the remainder of the feather toward the eye, tie off and repeat this procedure with the second feather. The hackle is now complete, PHOTO 202.

5. A couple of comments need to be made concerning what you have just accomplished. First, be sure to wind the feathers as closely as possible to the wings. If they are spread out too far away from the wings, you will tend to shorten the body behind and crowd the head

forward. Both situations reflect carelessness, but crowding the head can create an agony none of us wish to endure.

202

Secondly, I personally like to wind the hackle in a ratio of approximately two turns behind the wings to three turns in front. Obviously not all feathers will produce an even five turns, so you'll have to make the proper adjustments for the feathers you're using. This ratio gives the fly a balanced appearance both on, and off, the water.

L - HACKLING AROUND SPENT WINGS

The procedure here is the same as for hackling around upright wings, with the exception of the manner in which we tie the quills to the shank prior to winding the feathers.

203

Rather than laying the quill butts against the *side* of the hook, you'll set them down on *top* of the hook between the wings, PHOTO 203. The winds of thread both in front of, and behind the wings, will allow the quills to stay on *top* of the shank. The winds and tie-offs will be identical to the upright wings.

Chapter Eight: Additional Thoughts & Techniques

This chapter is devoted to those ideas, techniques and tying aids which didn't fall directly into the discussions of the previous chapters. They should not be considered as secondary in importance to the material already covered, but, to the contrary, will explain items of different technique which will complement your present knowledge.

A NON-TIP CEMENT BOTTLE

One problem all tiers are faced with is that of spilling an open bottle of head cement onto the tying table. It's easy to do, but not so easy to clean up! When I tie flies, I merely set the lid on top of the bottle without screwing it down tight after each use. Without proper precaution, it takes very little careless effort to bump the bottle, spilling its sticky contents onto the table, tools and materials.

A very effective method of preventing this annoyance is to epoxy a piece of cardboard or plastic to the bottom of the bottle, PHOTO 204. In so doing you have put the center of gravity right down near the table top.

204

Another method would be to set the bottle into a hole in a shallow box or small piece of board, PHOTO 204. These bases again lower the center of gravity to a point where it's almost impossible to tip the bottle. I prefer the epoxy and cardboard method because it requires less space on the table.

THE AFTER-TIE

You've just finished tying a fly. You've applied a coat of head cement and now you'll remove the fly from the vise to replace it with a bare hook for your next fly. What do you do with the completed fly with the wet head? Drop it on the table or into a small container just to have the wet cement attach itself to a small wisp of material on another fly? Certainly not!

When the fly is complete, hang it onto or stick it into something which will hold the wet head clear of anything to which it might adhere. Some tiers extend a wire somewhere near at hand and hang the hook bends from the wire. Others place blocks or strips of cork or foam on the table and stick the point of the completed fly into that material for drying.

For flies of size 16 and larger, I personally hang the bend over the lip of a thin cardboard box, PHOTO 205. I can place about two dozen flies around the box and the heads hang free from any loose material which could stick to them. The flies are easily placed, and easily removed.

205

WEIGHTING WET FLIES

It's often advantageous to add weight to the shank of a hook to facilitate quicker and deeper penetration of the fly into the water. The most common and effective method of doing this is to wrap the shank with lead wire.

The wire used is known as "fuse wire" and is readily available from material suppliers. There are four sizes (diameters) of wire which are practical for use on flies. They are designated 1/2 amp, 1 amp, 2 amp and 4 amp. A reasonable hook size range for each wire size is as follows:

1/2 amp - size #18 and smaller
1 amp - size #10 to #16
2 amp - size #2 to #8
4 amp - larger than #2

A - THE WEIGHTING PROCEDURE–ROUND PROFILE

1. Cover the shank with a layer of thread. This helps prevent the wire from rolling around the shank after tied.

2. Cut, or break, a section of lead wire about three inches long. CAUTION: When using your scissors to cut lead wire, gold wire, tinsel, etc. do not use the very tips of the scissors as cutting these metal materials will dull the cutting edges. Always cut down about 1/2 inch or more from the tips.

3. Coat the middle section of the hook shank with head cement. With your tying thread hanging back at the tail, set the lead wire down on top of the shank with your left thumb and index finger close to the shank, PHOTO 206.

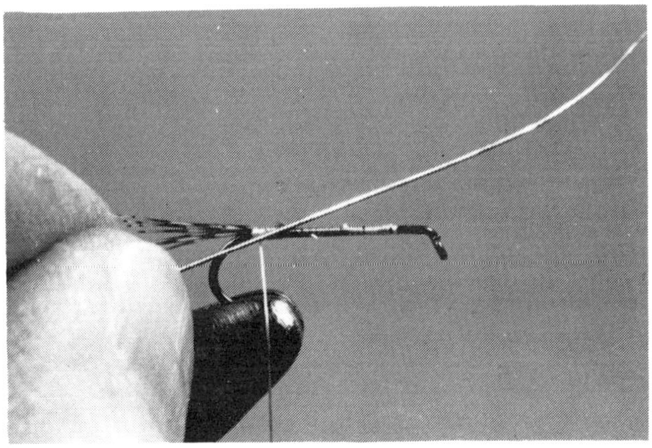

206

4. Now merely wind the wire forward with your right hand until you have applied as much wire as you desire. You may use as little as you wish, but don't overdo it when you want a lot of weight. Leave some room in front of the tail and behind the eye to accommodate the tying in of other materials and finishing off the head. PHOTO 207 shows the limits of shank coverage when maximum weight is desired.

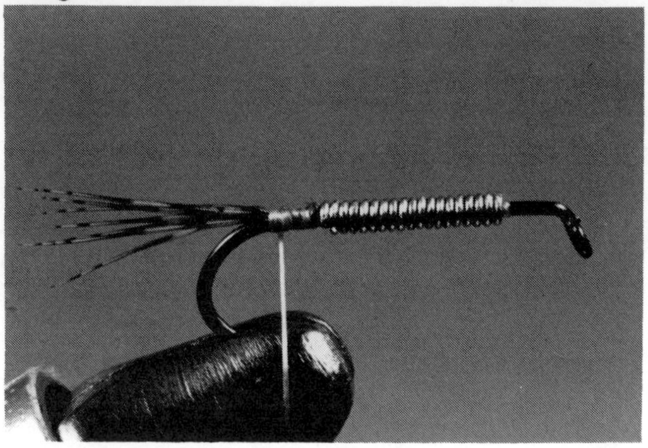

207

B - THE WEIGHTING PROCEDURE—FLAT PROFILE

When you wish the body of a nymph to be relatively flat in cross-section, this end can be easily accomplished while the fly is being weighted. Rather than winding the lead wire *around* the hook shank, it is laid against both sides of the shank. Should you not wish the fly to be weighted, but still desire the flat appearance, nylon leader material can be used in lieu of the lead wire.

1. Cut a piece of lead wire or monofilament approximately twice as long as the hook shank being used. The diameter of this material should be close to the diameter of the hook shank wire.

2. Cover the shank with a closely wound base of thread. Let the thread hang slightly to the left of the eventual front-end of the body. Lay one end of the wire along the far side of the shank with the front end of the wire at the point where the thread hangs, and the other end extending to your left.

3. With relatively loose turns, wind the thread to your left and bind the wire to the shank. These winds will go back to about mid-shank, PHOTO 208. If you wind too tightly, you may roll the wire underneath the shank!

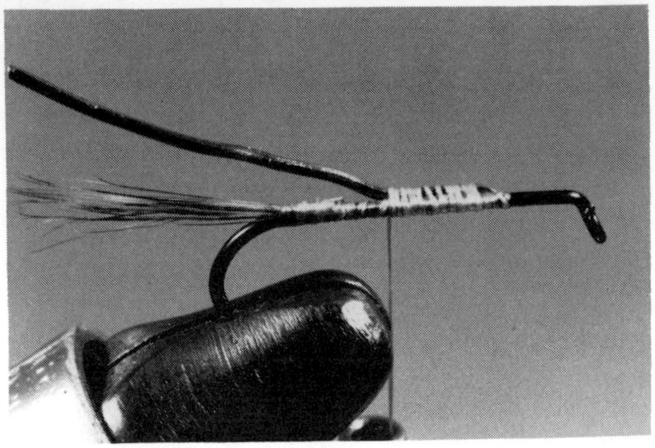

208

4. Now loop the wire to bring its free end along your side of the shank and even with the first end tied in. Wind the thread forward to bind the wire to your side of the shank, PHOTO 209.

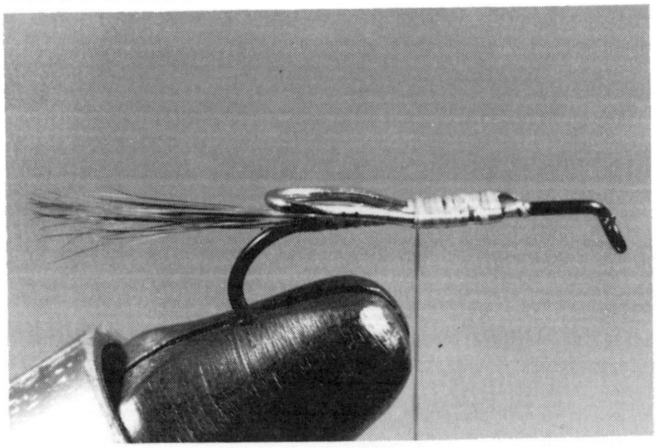

209

5. Cut off the loop at the point which will give you maximum weight, but also allow enough room to accommodate forming a taper of the body material at the tail.

6. Wind the thread around both sections of wire, holding them with the left hand to assure they stay on the *sides* of the shank. When you have them bound into place, cover the thread, wires and shank with head cement to keep them permanently in position, PHOTO 210. You're now ready to wind a body of your choice.

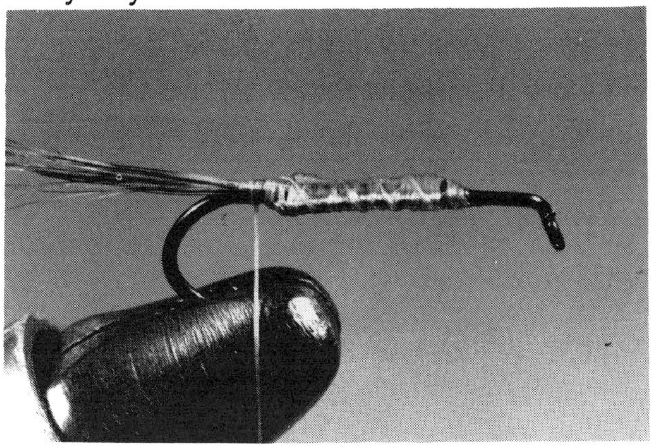

210

EXTENDED BODIES

The long mayfly body tied out beyond the bend of the hook is not a dressing tied frequently by most tiers, but it is one we may wish to tie occasionally. Several different materials may be used as the "core" of the extension, but most frequently it is nothing more than a section of nylon monofilament leader material. The outer body materials are those we would normally use in dressing directly to the hook shank, with one exception being clipped deer hair which would present tying problems to an impractical degree. For purposes of practice, let's tie the body of the extended Light Cahill pattern. For greater photographic clarity, I have omitted placing the wings as the first application of materials, although this would normally be done when tying a complete fly.

1. Cover the back half of the shank of a #12 dry fly hook with tying thread. This base will help prevent the monofilament core from turning on the shank. Let the thread hang just behind the normal wing position.

2. Cut a section of 15 pound test monofilament about 1-1/2 inches long. Place a drop of head cement along the top of the base thread. Set the mono down on the top of the shank and secure tightly. When placing the mono into position, be sure it extends either straight back or curved slightly upward, PHOTO 211.

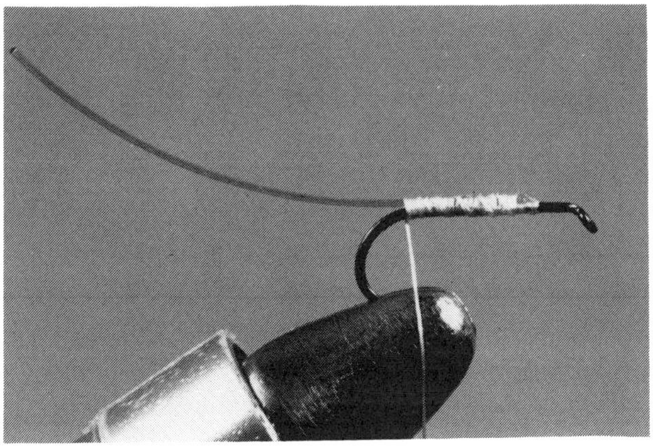

211

3. Wind thread up the mono to the point at which you want the body to terminate. When making these winds, you may wish to do so with your left hand; or if that proves to be too awkward, rotate the vise post 180 degrees so the tail is now extending to your *right* and use your right hand to wind. If you pursue the latter option, be sure to wind the thread *toward* you in a counter-clockwise direction when viewed from the right. Half hitch the thread here and coat this entire core-thread with cement to help keep the winds from slipping down or off the mono.

4. Select about a dozen cream colored hackle fibers and tie in for the tail, PHOTO 212. Apply a thin coat of cement over these winds.

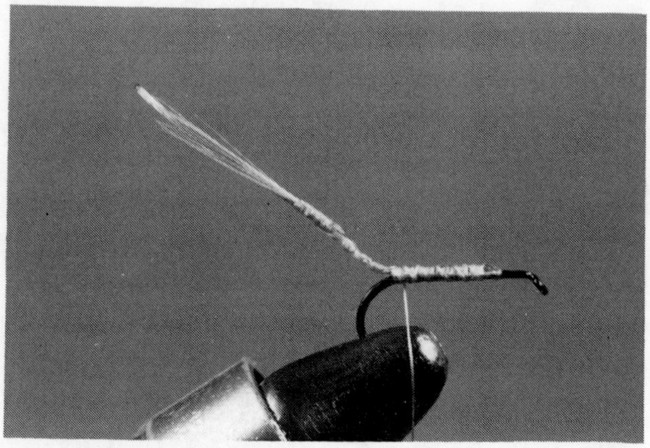

212

5. Dub cream colored fur or synthetic dubbing material to about four inches of your tying thread and wind the body. Just prior to winding, apply a thin coat of cement to the monofilament core. Start with a small diameter body at the tail and progressively increase its size until you reach the wings (not shown), PHOTO 213.

213

6. Cut the excess mono with scissors or fingernail clippers just beyond the body under the tail. Be absolutely certain you don't cut any of the thread winds or tail fibers. That's it! The extended body is complete. It took longer to tie than a standard body, but it looks good and you've learned another technique. These bodies may be ribbed and other materials may be utilized, but the basic procedure is the same.

ANTENNAE

Some fly patterns can be tied with a better representative quality if they include fibers to imitate the antennae of the natural insect. Depending on the materials used, the antennae can be extremely delicate to represent that of a small adult insect, or somewhat stout to represent that of a large nymph. Materials may include the very delicate fibers of a hackle feather or body feather, the more durable quill portion of one of these feathers, or stiff sections of nylon monofilament.

For our sample here, we'll tie with partridge body feather fibers.

1. The fly has been completely tied with the exception of forming the head. Inspect the feather and select the position on the quill from which the desired length of fibers emerge. Below this point, use your scissors to trim the fibers to within 1/16 inch of the quill, for 1/4 inch down the quill. These tiny stubs of fiber will help prevent the quill from moving when it's tied into the fly. Now with the points of your scissors, cut the quill immediately above the two bottom-most fibers, PHOTO 214. These two fibers will be your antennae.

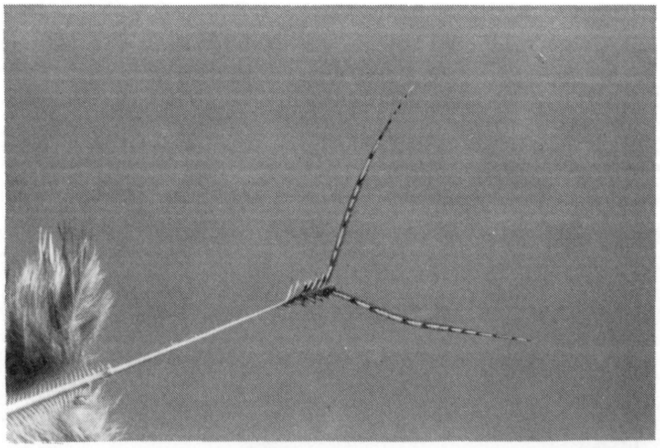

214

2. Set the quill down on the head area of the fly and secure with tying thread. Taper head as usual, trim the quill butt, and whip finish

the head. This procedure is similar to the four fiber split tail except we use only two fibers.

When using hackle quill, monofilament or some other material where two individual antenna are desired, merely set and secure separately.

GILLS ON NYMPHS

Sometimes it's effective to embellish a fly body with an extra, added attraction. One such technique might be the addition of gills along the sides of the abdomen on a nymph pattern. Gills of the natural insects are extremely delicate and a good representation can be produced with the use of ostrich or peacock herl. For practice, let's use the ostrich herl. In purchasing ostrich herl, we ask for a section of ostrich "plume." The plume is similar in appearance to the peacock "stick" we used for the peacock quill and herl bodies.

1. With the tail in place, tie in a desired material for a rib. In the photo I have used thread.

2. Tie in sections of ostrich quill by the tip ends on each side of the shank, extending to the left beyond the tail, PHOTO 215.

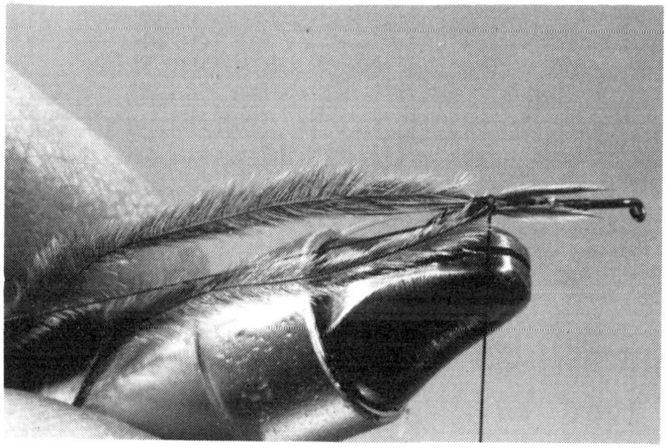

215

3. Build up a body of floss. One at a time, pull the quills forward and tie down so they lay along the *sides* of the body. Be sure the quills are pulled *tightly* forward as you tie them down.

4. Wind the rib material forward around the gills and body, being careful to assure the gills remain along the sides of the body and protrude out at a right angle. Tie off the rib and trim away the excess. You now have tied a good representation of nymph gills, PHOTO 216.

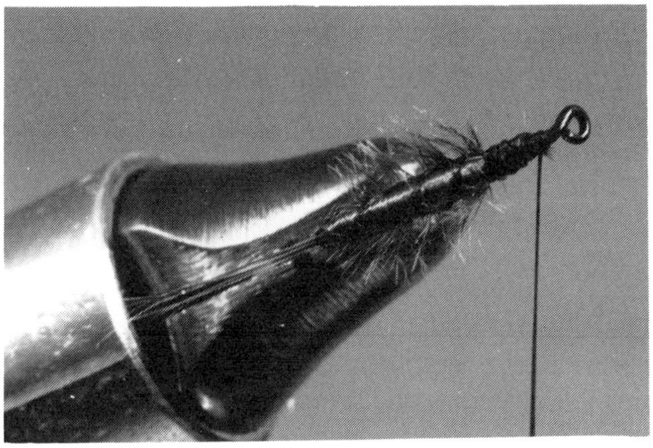

216

TYING SCUDS

This crustacean is also referred to as a fresh water shrimp. Though they are in fact different creatures, their general conformation is similar and therefore their artificial imitations are tied in a similar manner. The two main features predominant on most imitations are the "shell back" or "backstrap," and the many legs directly under the body. I'll briefly describe a typical tying procedure using two different styles of leg representations.

1. Because the body shape is normally an arched configuration, scuds are most

frequently tied on a bait hook (Mustad #37160). In the photographs, I have used the Mustad in size #14. If less arc is desired this hook can be bent more open with pliers, or a normal long hook with a straight shank could be bent into a curve with pliers.

2. Cover the shank with a base of thread and tie in a hackle fiber tail. Tie in a ribbing material where you tied down the tail. (I've used gold wire.) At that same position tie in a backstrap material. (Here I've used a piece of clear plastic bag folded a couple of times to a width of about 1/8 inch.) Other materials commonly used for the backstrap are latex rubber, raffia, nylon raffia, animal hair, etc. If the fly is to be weighted, wind the lead wire around the shank after tying in the backstrap, PHOTO 217.

217

3. I prefer to use dubbed fur for the body as it has a good translucent quality. When the fur is blended with Orlon or antron yarn fibers, even more translucency is derived. Dub and wind the body so it is relatively thick along the front half of the shank. For this particular dubbing, I prefer to use the dubbing tool method. As you wind the body you may find it more convenient to change the position of the hook in the vise once or twice to prevent the thread from falling off the shank. Now pluck out the fibers on the underside of the body with your bodkin point. These long, loose fibers will represent the legs. Your thread now hangs at the front end of the body.

4. Pull the backstrap forward to lay over the topside of the body and secure it to the shank. Wind the rib forward and secure. Again with your bodkin, pluck the leg fibers out until they are good and fuzzy! Finish the head and the fly is complete, PHOTO 218.

218

The second legging method utilizes a hackle feather palmered the length of the body instead of the body-plucking technique.

1. After tying in the tail, rib, and backstrap, tie in the tip of a proper size hackle feather (1-1/2 to 2 gaps long). You may want to experiment here by using a feather from which you have removed the fiber from one side of the quill. If this is your choice, use two feathers.

219

2. Dub and wind a fur or synthetic fur body. Wind the hackle forward and tie off. Cut the hackle fibers from the top and sides of the body allowing only the bottom fibers to extend as legs beneath the body, PHOTO 219.

3. Pull the backstrap over and tie off. Wind the rib and tie off. Finish the head. If any leg fibers were tied under or bent out of position by the rib material, re-align them with your bodkin point. Cement the head and the scud is complete, PHOTO 220.

220

NYMPHS—THEIR LEGS AND WING CASES

You already possess the skills required to tie the tails and bodies of nymphs. In PHOTO 221, I have shown an incomplete stonefly nymph which includes the tail, the abdomen (dark fur), the thorax (light fur, larger in diameter than the abdomen to properly represent the natural insect), and a rib over the abdomen. The legs are missing as is the wing case (sometimes referred to as "wing pad(s)" and "covert(s)"). These two components will be discussed in this section. To start with, let's learn a legging method.

221

A - HACKLE FIBER LEGS

This form of nymph leg structure is the easiest of the two methods we'll discuss.

1. After you have completed ribbing the abdomen for a stonefly nymph on a #8, #79580 hook, and before building the thorax, tie in a long, one-sided hackle feather by the *tip*, PHOTO 222.

222

2. Build a complete thorax and allow the thread to hang at its forward end.

3. With your hackle pliers wind the feather forward, palmer style, to the front of the thorax and tie off, PHOTO 223.

4. With your scissors trim away the fibers extending upward and downward from the thorax, so that the remaining fibers now extend only to the sides to represent the

laterally extended legs of the actual nymph under water, PHOTO 224. This completes this style of legging. The second style is described in paragraph "C", but you'll want to continue now to paragraph "B."

223

224

B - THE FREE WING CASE(S)

This case representation is secured to the fly only at the front end of the case. The material used is usually a feather, but may also be formed from latex, leather, plastic, etc. The latter materials are available in a flat "sheet" form and the case would be cut to appropriate shape with scissors or a blade and then tied to the hook. For our practice here, we'll use a partridge body feather which requires a more involved procedure than that required when cutting a wing case from sheet material. The color desired will determine the feather used. Brown is very common, so we'll use partridge. In the photographs, I have already tied the tail, abdomen, thorax and hackle fiber legs.

1. Prepare a brown partridge feather as you did for the flat downwing but pulling it between the tips of your left thumb and index finger which are coated with a drop of head cement. Allow the feather to dry *slightly* wider than the width of your thorax.

2. Physically or visually measure the length of the thorax and with the quill of the feather held by the left thumb and index finger, cut the feather off so its length is slightly longer than the thorax. With your scissors, cut a V out of the now square tip end of the feather, PHOTO 225.

225

226

3. With your bodkin point, place a drop of *thick* head cement on the top of the thorax. Set the prepared feather down on top of the

thorax with the concave side of the feather facing downward and secure as in PHOTO 226. Press down on the case for a few moments to allow the cement to bond the case to the thorax. Finish the head as usual and the fly is complete.

Natural mayfly larvae have but one wing case. Stonefly larvae have two cases and many tiers prefer to tie a second case on these artificials. This is easily done as follows:

1. In step one above, prepare two glazed feathers rather than one.

2. In step two, cut one feather as described and the second feather slightly shorter, but also with the V cut out.

3. In step three, place the first feather as described and the shorter feather on top of the first with a drop of cement between them, PHOTO 227. Allow a space to remain between the bottom case and the loose end of the top case. In other words, cement only the front half of the top case to the bottom case. The double wing case is complete.

227

C - THE FOLD-OVER LEGS AND FOLDOVER WING CASE

The procedures which follow are more complicated than those discussed for the previous legs and case, but in my opinion present the body parts in a more durable and life-like imitation of the natural insect.

The fold-over method described here will present the legs and wing case simultaneously because of the sequential orientation in which they are necessarily tied. We'll use a brown partridge hackle feather for both the case and the legs.

1. Before you begin with the feather preparation, wind the abdomen and the rib on a #8, #79580 hook. Select two partridge feathers. Featherglaze one of the feathers with the finger-tip method, forming its width slightly wider than the thorax will be.

2. When the feather is dry, place it down on the shank, concave side up, with the tip of the feather pointing to your right. Wind the tying thread around both the feather tip and the shank to secure the tip immediately in front of the abdomen. Make sure the tips of the fibers which originate closest to the butt end of the quill are being secured to the hook as you wind, PHOTO 228. This feather will form your wing case.

228

3. The second feather does not receive a featherglaze. Strip all the downy material and fuzzy fibers from the butt of the stem. Physically or visually measure the distance between the abdomen and the eye of the hook. Holding the tip in your right hand, with the feather concave side up and the bare

quill butt pointing to your left, measure this *same* distance from the place where the butt-end fibers start toward the tip of the feather. Pull the fibers within this distance to your left so they lay back toward the butt end of the quill. PHOTO 229 shows the fibers pulled to the left.

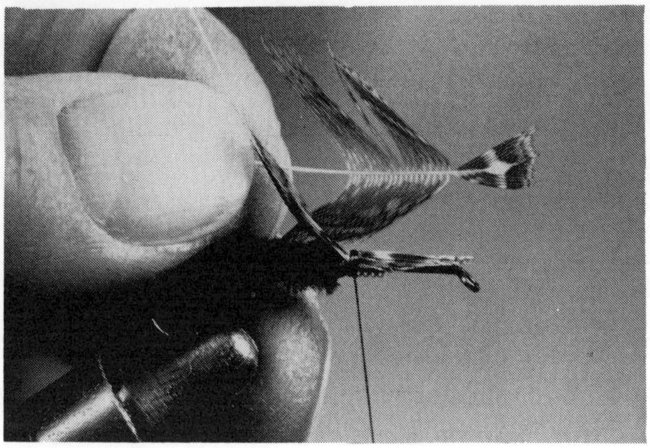

229

4. Set this feather down on the hook in the same manner you did the wing case feather, i.e. tip to the right and concave side up. Now secure the feather at the same point on the shank at which you secured the first feather, with the thread winding over the quill at the point where the fibers change directions, PHOTO 230. Now cut off the fibers protruding to the right. This feather will form the legs.

230

5. Build the thorax and allow the thread to hang at its forward end (don't crowd the head with the thorax). With your right hand grasping the quill, pull the "leg" feather forward over the top of the thorax, secure by winding with the left hand, PHOTO 231, and trim away the excess.

231

6. With your left thumb and forefinger press down on the fibers so they are somewhat equally spaced along the length of the thorax. Place a drop or two of cement on the quill and fibers along the top of the thorax to secure the fibers and quill to the thorax. This procedure will help prevent the legs from bunching up in one location when the wing case is positioned.

7. Grasp the remaining feather with the right hand, pull forward over the thorax and secure as you did the leg feather. Trim away excess, finish off the head and you now have a nymph tied with foldover legs and a foldover wing case, PHOTO 232. For added durability, apply a coat of cement to the wing case as you cement the head.

232

Other materials commonly used on this type of case are plastic and latex. Merely cut them to proper width, tie in, fold over and tie off as you did the partridge feather. I personally like to use yarn for wing cases. Depending on its size, four to eight strands of yarn can be tied in before the leg feather is set, and the case will then be completed as above. It's very durable, somewhat translucent, has good bulk, comes in many colors and can be barred or striped as desired with a permanent ink marking pen.

233

KNOTS FOR KNEES

There may be times when you'll want to put individual legs on larger sized patterns, such as stonefly nymphs and grasshoppers, and it's possible to add a slightly greater touch of reality in these situations by putting a joint in the leg. The procedure is simple. In PHOTO 233 a simple overhand knot was tied in the trimmed hackle quill (right), the goose quill, and the small bundle of ringneck pheasant tail feather fibers. PHOTO 234 illustrates how the right end of the leg material being used is pulled over itself to form a circular loop. It is held in this position between the left thumb and index finger. Tweezer points are then pushed downward through the loop to grasp the end of the material. When the tweezer points are retracted back up through the loop, the knot tightens and the leg joint is formed.

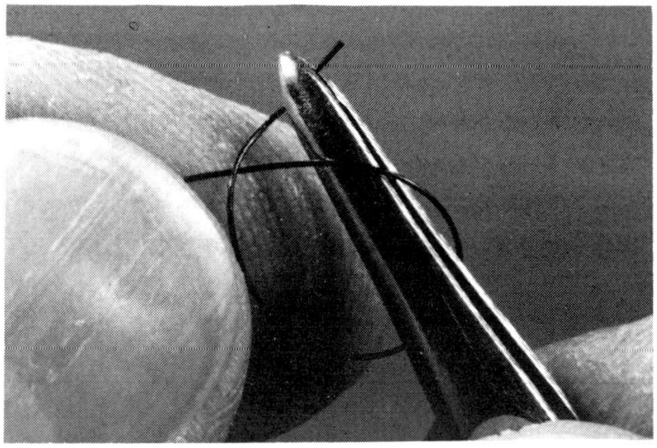

234

A WEED GUARD

Under certain angling conditions a fly protected from collecting weeds and moss on the point of the hook is a great blessing. One method of helping to avoid this problem is the incorporation of a "bumper" or guard in front of the hook point.

This method, which is easy to tie, has the advantage of using relatively transparent monofilament nylon.

235

1. After tying in the tail, tie in a short section of monofilament along the side of the shank,

extending to the rear, as in PHOTO 235. The size of the mono will vary with the size of the hook. Material of eight pound test works well on #12 hooks.

2. After the fly has been completed, except for winding the head, pull the mono forward to curve around the bend and tie it in under the head, PHOTO 236. (The fly in the photo is not complete.) This guard is certainly not weed *proof*, but it helps!

236

REMOVING PEACOCK EYE HERL

As mentioned in the section on tying peacock quill bodies, the quills of the eye itself are short in length, but have a very nice longitudinal color variance which is advantageous when a distinct segmented appearance is desired. The main drawback in using these quills is the difficulty encountered when removing the herl with your thumb nail or an eraser. With little effort, however, the herl can be removed efficiently as follows.

In a saucepan, melt three or four cakes of paraffin. When the paraffin is in a liquid but not boiling state, immerse the entire peacock eye into the liquid, remove immediately, and set aside to cool and solidify. With each herl-covered quill now covered with the solid paraffin, it's an easy task to strip the herl from individual quills with your thumb nail just as you did with the unwaxed quills.

CONCLUSION

You have just covered a lot of ground! You have waded through the words and photos of a different world from that you knew before you were bitten by the fly tying bug. I hope the semantic current didn't knock you off your feet.

My main hope, of course, is that you stuck with it, endured the tedium of practicing all the procedures presented, and now possess the skill and desire to learn even more about fly tying.

I hope you feel you've learned to tie well, and with relative ease; for that was my purpose in writing this book and writing it in the manner I did. You have now mastered the basics and will be able to understand the more advanced techniques presented by other sources. These other sources may also amplify or improve what has been presented here, but what is most important is the fact that you are now a fly tier.

You have a new talent, and expanded vocabulary, and another avenue through which you will make new friends and acquaintances. Believe me, you can do a lot worse than having fly tiers and fly fishermen as your friends. I've been around them for many years and they're my favorite kind of people.

For a closing remark I want to wish you the very best in whatever direction fly tying takes you and, if that direction brings you pleasure, I'm proud to have played some small part in making it happen.

RECOMMENDED BOOKS FOR YOUR FURTHER FLY TYING DEVELOPMENT

American Nymph Fly Tying Manual - Randall Kaufmann
Dressing Flies For Fresh and Salt Water - Poul Jorgensen
The Essential Fly Tier - J. Edson Leonard
Flies - J. Edson Leonard
The Fly Tyer's Almanac - Robert Boyle and Dave Whitlock
Fly Tying Materials - Eric Leiser
Master Fly Tying Guide - Art Flick
Matching The Hatch - Ernest Schwiebert
Modern Fly Dressings For the Practical Angler - Poul Jorgensen
Nymphs - Ernest Schwiebert
Popular Fly Patterns - Terry Hellekson
Selective Trout - Doug Swisher and Carl Richards
Streamer Fly Tying and Fishing - Joseph Bates, Jr.
Western Trout Fly Tying Manual - Jack Dennis

MATERIALS DIRECTORY

A wide variety of materials may be used to dress the separate components of artificial flies. The most common natural and manufactured materials are listed here to give you a general overview of what they are. This is by no means a complete listing because the materials you may use are limited only by your imagination and the material availability.

If you have access to a retail store selling tying materials, visit with the staff and look over their displays. Fly tiers are usually very willing to share their know-how with others and you can learn a great deal merely by asking questions and physically examining the materials.

Most materials are quite reasonably priced. As your budget permits, purchase a material or two which interests you and experiment with it on the hook shank. I'm sure most all tiers have gone through an initial stage of experimentation and "creative tying," and most of us continue with this inclination. We learn what can be done, what presumably can't be done, what might be done, what's practical and impractical, and sometimes we discover a material or technique which spurs us on to a new stage of experimentation and creativity.

As with fly fishing itself, fly tying continues to offer a lifetime of challenges and opportunities. There's always something new to learn!

The materials for fly tying are usually classified in, but by no means limited to, the following categories:

FEATHERS

A - Hackle Necks, Dry Fly and Wet Fly

B - Body Feathers (Plumage)

Golden Pheasant
Grouse
Guinea Hen
Mallard Duck
Mandarin Duck
Marabou
Ostrich
Partridge
Teal Duck
Woodduck

QUILLS

Duck Wing
Goose Wing
Hackle Neck
Javalina
Moose Mane
Peacock
Pheasant Tail
Porcupine
Turkey Wing & Tail

HAIR

Bear
Bucktail
Caribou
Deer Body
Elk
Kip Tail
Mink Tail
Moose
Polar Bear
Skunk
Squirrel Tail

TINSELS

Embossed
Flat
Oval
Gold & Silver Wire
Mylar Piping

DUBBING FUR

Australian Opossum
Beaver
Chinchilla
Fox
Hare's Mask
Mink
Mole
Otter
Muskrat
Rabbit
Seal
Synthetic Materials

CONTINUOUS STRAND MATERIALS

Antron
Crewel Yarn
Chenille
Floss
Mohair
Mohlon
Polypropylene
Spun Fur
Thread
Wool Yarn

INDEX

TO OUR READERS

In some regions of the country specialized books such as ours are most easily purchased via mail order. Whether for your own library, or that of a friend, we want our books to be available to you when you want them; therefore, we include this order form for your convenience.

ORDER FORM

Please send me the following books published by Stream Stalker, Inc.

Qty.	TITLE	Price	Total
________	Fly Tying 101	$18.95	________
________	The Colorado Angling Guide	$24.95	________
________	The Montana Angling Guide	$24.95	________
________	The Wyoming Angling Guide	$24.95	________
________	Rocky Mountain Trilogy (One of each Angling Guide in an attractive slip case)	$72.00	________

Sub-Total ________

Tax: 3% for Colorado residents ________

Shipping & Handling $ 3.00

TOTAL DUE $ ________

(Please print)

Name ________________________________

Address (for UPS shipment) ________________________________

City/State/Zip ________________________________

Check or M.O. Enclosed ________ MasterCard ________ Visa ________

Card Account Number ________________ Exp. Date ________

Signature ________________________________

Autographed Copies Requested ________

Send Order To:

Stream Stalker, Inc.
P.O. Box 238
Woody Creek, CO 81656
(303) 923-4552

NOTES

NOTES